The Star Crossed Serpent
Volume II

"*Fire as such is the province of the Alder (tree), the god of the Underworld - Time -* that which creates and destroys the world of appearances - finally Bran or Brian/Baal, the god of Fire, of Craft, of lower magic and fertility and death. All things that are of this world belong to him, the Star-Crossed Serpent. So you come to *the true meaning of the cauldron. Bring forth the star-son, and you have Dionysus,* the horn child and Jesus Christ in one."

Robert Cochrane

The Star Crossed Serpent
Vol II

The Clan of Tubal Cain
The Legacy Continues: Shani Oates (1998 -

by

Shani Oates
(Chapters 1-10)
Epilogue: Robin-the-Dart

Copyright © 2012 Mandrake & Shani Oates
ISBN
First edition hardback 2012

All rights reserved. No part of this work may be reproduced or utilized in any form by any means, electronic or mechanical, including *xerography, photocopying, microfilm*, and *recording*, or by any information storage system without permission in writing from the publishers.

Published by
Mandrake of Oxford
PO Box 250
OXFORD
OX1 1AP (UK)

Other books by Shani Oates and available from Mandrake:
Tubelo's Green Fire: Mythos, Ethos, Female, Male and Priestly Mysteries of The Clan of Tubal Cain, isbn 978-1-906958-07-7

The Arcane Veil: Witchcraft and Occult Science from the People of the Dark-ages to the People of Goda, of the Clan of Tubal Cain.
978-1-906958-35-0 (£25/$40 hbk)

For Val

SKETCH OF ROY - HALCYON DAYS

Table of Contents

The Legacy Today: Shani Oates 1998-

     Intro: The Ring Troth of Cain 9
1. The Archer's Song 11
2. Brimstone & Treacle 22
3. The Faith of the Wise 49
4. The Stang 66
5. The 4th Nail 106
6. Dark Aegipan and Pale Leukothea 114
7. Cain and Craft Diversity 122
8. Cain, Clanship and the Egregore 135
9. Patterns of Transformation: the Alchemy of Being 160
10. The Poison Chalice 172
     Epilogue 183
     Notes 187
     Bibliography & Index 199

List of Illustrations:

Sketch of Roy - Halcyon Days 6
Sumerian cylinder seals – archaic staffs 68
Roy's Star Stang – Clan Cosmology 72
Lady of the Sycamore 76
Four Nails 107
Star, Hammer & Sickle Glyph 133
Clan Insignia 171
Poisoned Chalice [after John] 182

Introduction:
The Ring Troth of Cain

After all had gathered at the (*Gardh* Tree)[1] 'Council Tree' Odhin presents his Hero:

Thor pronounces: "*I decree that he be childless, the last of his race.*"

Odhin responds: "*I grant him life three times the length of mortal man.*"

Thor returns: "*I destine him to do in each age a grievous outrage that shall be a work of shame and dishonour in the eyes of man.*"

Odhin counters: "*I bestow upon him the stoutest armour and most precious garments.*"

Thor answers: "*I forbid him both house and home, nor shall a piece of land ever be his.*"

Odhin retorts: "*I allot him gold and flocks in fullest plenty.*"

Thor answers: "*Then I doom him to ever growing thirst for gold and wealth, that he may never enjoy peace of mind.*"

Odhin replies: "*I confer on him valour and prowess, and victory in battle.*"

Thor adds: "*Yet shall he from each combat bear a wound that reaches to the very bone.*"

Odhin says: "*The noble law of the skalds shall be his, that he may sing, and each of his words shall be a song.*"

Thor Says: "*His memory shall be cursed with forgetfulness, of all that he has sung.*"

Odhin declares: "*But the noblest and best among men shall love and honour him.*"

Thor's parting curse: "*But all his tribe shall shun and hate him.*"

(W. Wagner)

1 The Archer's Song: Are Nursery Rhymes Child's Play?

Robert Cochrane was known to be fond of rhymes, poems, songs and prayers. All grist for the Mill and all with a homily to reveal; in fact his consummate skills at punning and double entendre are legendary. In that genre he was ahead of his time and in good company. The clues he felt, were as ever, hidden in plain sight!

Nursery Rhymes, we are told, are for children. Not so, challenges Norman Iles, who rather boldly declares them to be thinly disguised risqué poetry in his innovative and refreshing study of a selection of the most popular examples.[2] Contentious yet entertaining, his critique offers a very credible and plausible purpose in their apparent descent into nonsense and ambiguity. Though his provocative conclusions may not please conservative folklorists, his challenging wit proffers food for thought. The real meanings, he insists are veiled euphemistically in order to avoid the censure of the Obscenity Laws in operation prior to 1963.

His research unearthed countless 'bowdlerized' versions of the more popular rhymes that shame the most strident rugby songs! With tongue firmly-in-cheek, Iles offers restored versions, sourced from selected extant remnants, tendering considerable variety in expressions and form. This should, at the very least force us to reconsider how we examine such materials with a view to re-evaluating defunct terminologies, a primary example of which is – 'nursery,' especially as a descriptive typology. Iles insists the content is certainly not suitable for those of tender years, adding that subtleties become lost after only two generations, exposing only literal intent and taken often at face value. Anomalies invite interpretation, but this seldom reaches into the heart and origin of the subject matter. Worse, he bemoans, they are reviewed through a distorted lens subject to nostalgia, which assumes impossibly romanticized perspectives as primary examples pertinent to a more enchanted period of mystical awareness.

In fact, rhymes as records of legendary or historical events are, he insists, highly improbable. Otherwise, he argues, why would good folk keep repeating them long after events wherein their relevance has expired? By way of compensation, he suggests that these novel themes are a constant, retaining a rude universality, a perverse continuity and a timeless fascination with all the vulgar aspects of human nature across the whole spectrum of class and privilege. The enduring human life cycle is after all what obsesses all folk custom encompassing births, marriage, romance, death and the humours of life itself. This is folk custom at its basest and possibly most honest. It is he says, the kind of stuff we discover scrawled on the back of toilet doors, on school desks and pub trivia sheets. Sex is often (though not exclusively) considered man's first instinct and this enthrallment with the body is clearly and for Iles, unambiguously reflected within the texts of these apparently 'innocent' rhymes.

The 'Archer's Song,' as a prime example is more commonly known by the title: *'Green Grow the Rushes O.'* This popular rhyme is one of several folk songs made significant by the context Robert Cochrane ascribed to it within several of his letters. He was fond of lateral analogy and this song may be proved as no exception to his genius. Iles, after noticing certain similarities in a number of the verses (4, 10, 11&12) to a well known hymn, speculates that its basic format could have provided the mandatory source for the rather pious *'New Dial.'* Here however, the tone becomes transmuted into very reverential praise of the evangelists, the commandments, martyrs and apostles, being typical of the whole rhyme.

It might be appropriate at this stage to see the standard version of this popular song:

I'll sing you one, O
Green grow the rushes, O
What is your one, O?
One is one and all alone
And evermore shall be so.

I'll sing you two, O
Green grow the rushes, O
What are your two, O?
Two, two, lily-white boys,
Clothed all in green, O
One is one and all alone
And evermore shall be so.

(Chorus: Two, two, lily-white boys
Clothed all in green, O

One is one and all alone
And evermore shall be so…)

Three, three - the rivals,

Four for the Gospel makers.

Five for the symbol (cymbals) at your door.

Six for the six proud walkers.

Seven for the seven stars in the sky.

Eight for the eight bold (April) rainers (or rangers).

Nine for the nine bright shiners.

Ten for the Ten Commandments.

Eleven for the eleven that went up to Heaven,

Twelve for the twelve Apostles.

In true Chaucerian fashion, Iles attempts to persuade us how the 'lily-white' pair is well, rather obvious in a Nell Gwynn kind of way, and the 'boys' are really a generic reference to 'things' rather more feminine than their name suggests. Clothed all 'in green' signifies the vigour of youth et cetera, in like fashion in ever increasing bawdiness, to talk of four buttocks in bed, five fingers and six as a measurement for alleged vigour, seven references 'ploughing,' eight, the act of insemination, nine the months of conception, and so on until when we reach ten, completion, where we start all over again. Eleven and twelve he states as simply misplaced interpolations.[62] Here then, is Iles' 'restored' version:

"I'll sing you one - O

Green grow the rushes - O

What is your one - O?

One is One and all alone

And ever more shall be so!

I'll sing you two - O

What is your Two - O?

Two, two, the lily-white lambs,

Clothed all in green – O

And so on: Three, three the ribald's; four for the merry makers; five for the fiddlers at your door; six, for the six proud standers; seven for the plough that's in the sky; eight for the April raining; nine for the nine bright shining months and ten for the new beginnings. Of course, though hilariously funny, this is the least likely of all the restored rhymes within Iles' book (which includes a very good version of Cock Robin and the Holly and the Ivy) and yet the very human element is so very compelling.

Another variant of the rhyme alleged to be '*The Archer's Song*'[a] is certainly relevant to the elusive teachings of Robert Cochrane as speculated by those who have studied his few writings, some of which suggest a more mystical missive overlaying the simple folk rhyming form:

One as the Monadic essence, the Supreme and indivisible Creatrix.

Two as the dyadic and/or Tanist twins – Holly and Oak kings, or Cain and Abel.

Three suggests the Triune Fates, or Theriomorphic Hekate, divine feminine triplicity.

Four is speculated as being the Four Castles, Kings or Queens of the Wind Gods, or even the Cardinal Elements. Yet again, it may be the Virtue of the 'Word,' breathed across each totem of the Four Cardinal Winds.

Five may allude to the figure of Cain in the main stars of Böötes; though five would better suggest the pentagrammatic hand that reveals the round of life through youth, maturity, death and rebirth, but more specifically, rather than one splayed hand as a warding symbol upon your 'door' the all important five separate but linked Clan keys or 'signs' given up at the gates that Robert Cochrane was known to use, passed between successive Magisters and used exclusively by them.

Six are fairly given as the six basic directions of a simple Compass (up, down, left right, fore and aft).

Seven are suggested in the stellar associations of the Plough, Cassiopeia and Draco.

Eight is given as the eightfold division of the year, the full Compass, but better I think would be the four pairs of guardians, or the seven+one potencies of the Underworld judges, angelic potencies, primal winds. Ancestral Hierarchies.

Nine could sensibly be the Muses, and/or the knots of the year, but they could also be the nine actual brightest stars of the Pleiades constellation, which figuratively if not literally, may or may not link them back in some way to the Muses.

Joe Wilson, a correspondent of Robert Cochrane's in the mid

sixties, offered his intuitive opinion of the song as *"a mnemonic device to help people to remember their 'catechism.'"*[5] After the traditional opening line, his poetic musings are as follows:

Two are found in a variant as *"the lily and the rose, that shine both red and green oh"* – these he explains as the winter and summer year kings of fecund green man and red hunter, both of whom become the lily white twins in death.

Three, he offers again as the Triple Goddess, whose reign is split across the solar year to four months each, beginning with November 1st.

Four he upholds as indicative of the Winds: Boreas –North; Notus – South; Eurus – East and Zephyrus - West, either in these forms or the Gods and Queens that represent them.

Five he identifies reasonably with the hand marked for the 'family' line and as a protection symbol at the door.

Six are discarnate teachers, the wanderers who traverse the oneiric dreamscapes.

Seven, he gives an interesting suggestion here as the 'Queen of Heaven' in relation to the Pleiades.

Joe Wilson left ***eight*** open to interpretation but added that one of his wives had considered the 'gabble ratchets'.

Nine he gives as the feasts of the year, for their bright fires. Others assert that he added three more verses to complete the set as follows: ***Ten*** for the 'Lady's Girdle'; ***Eleven*** for the 'Maidens in a Dance' and ***Twelve*** for the 'Wren in Ivy' which add their own poetry and worth.[6]

These astute observations offer plausible consideration of certain aspects of the Robert Cochrane teaching material, making any one theory as a singular legitimacy almost conceivable, that is, were it not for the scholarly versions more familiar to us. In one of these, it is claimed a Hebrew precedent of 'hoary' age authenticates it as a religious carol.[7]

One (again) refers unequivocally to God Almighty.

Two There is a suggestion here that these may refer to the two Hebrew Tables of the Law. Another version in which 'lilywhite maids' (minus their clothing of green) is not gender specific and which speculates the 'pair' alludes to Christ Jesus and St. John the Baptist.

Three encompasses many variants including 'drivers,' and 'divers' to name but two. There are no surviving terms that verify or justify the accepted association with the 'trinity'.

Four are the Christian authors of the gospels, similar in importance to the four patriarchs, throne angels and apocalyptic beasts of the Hebraic version.

Five is given many popular variations that range between magical symbols, to musical cymbals, being placed upon a door or threshold (with the implication of protection), the feet, or the hands.

Six receives considerable speculation, with suggestions of 'charmers' or 'waters' in place of 'walkers.' The eminent folklorist, Andrew Lang opines without real justification, that six bowls or jars of (charmed) water (oblique reference to Cana) are here inferred. Curiously, two untraceable and very obscure versions mention 'virtuous horses' and 'lamps were burning bright,' that do offer themselves to a more mystical interpretation.

Seven are the stars in the constellation of Ursa Major, known commonly as the 'Plough' or Gabriel's Wain. Other versions offer the 'seven liberal arts' from the 17th century or 'days of the week' in the Hebrew version.

Eight (bold) rangers become 'archangels,' though why is never made clear. A Seven plus one combination of archaic provenance perhaps? How tempting are such conclusions!

Nine 'bright shiners' become nine 'gable rangers', and have some connection to the eight archangels and the seven stars, all being consistent if obscure. Nine Muses are also given in one version.

Ten Commandments are unanimous, so could indeed be either a universal precedent or interpolation.

Eleven are the apostles minus Judas who betrayed Jesus, who for his alleged sin, did not ascend to Heaven with his brothers to become radiant (and in some version, myriad) stars in the firmament. Interestingly, a Berkshire version mentions 'Belshazzar's Horses,' which are professed to ride the skies as starry steeds.

Twelve apostles; again universal, except where they represent the Twelve Tribes of Israel in the Hebrew version.

The Twelve days of Christmas have even been suggested in this counting rhyme/carol/song which was first printed in full in its present known form in 'English County Songs: Words and Music' by Etheldred Broadwood and J.A. Fuller-Maitland in 1892, though this is challenged by the Scot's claim to a version in the late 18th century by Robert Burns.[8]

Other folklorists, unable or unwilling to separate one version from another accept all versions as valid to those who created, appropriated or amended them, each has merit and purpose and may be enjoyed and celebrated for it. In the true spirit of the 'Word,' all versions therefore retain 'truths' appropriate to those reading, singing or teaching them. And of course the more amusing observations highlight the disingenuous perspectives of those models deemed, 'superior.' Iles challenges us here to ask only that we relate popular songs to popular life, rather than to pious or lofty ideals, and there is some merit in this. He shifts us from the sacred to the profane.

Certainly, where Paganism is present in remnant form, rather than placed retrospectively, it is with regard to the spirit of the land and not to wistful pockets of secret religions, continuing oblivious to progress. This cycle of life is not incongruent with that offered within Christianity, following on the same customary themes and traditions with few changes. There is no contradiction. Neither too does any single adaptation offer greater merit or usefulness beyond other extant versions. In fact, this is one of the great attractions of folklore, the amazing variety of form, application and rationale.

So each season, whatever the tide, pause for just a moment to consider that in all things, there is always more than meets the eye and more than what is obvious or immediately apparent. Then celebrate life at *all* levels, sacred and profane. Seek the truth in the fullest expression of manifest creation; from the spark, the seed, the fruit, the bud and stem, the corn, to the mill, the oven and the loaf it collectively bakes.

Cumulatively, it *all* makes perfect sense. Sometimes we cannot see beyond our own kernel of truth, or perhaps more appropriately, the wheat for the chaff? Sometimes we need to lift our eyes from the page to see the words on the other side. In cunning lies the All. All is One and *"One is One and all alone and ever more shall be so…"*

2 Brimstone and Treacle

> "It is very improbable that the Devil, who being a wise and mighty spirit would be at the beck and call of a poor old hag. And to have so little to do as to attend to the errands and important lusts of silly old women." ('Saducimus Triumphatus' – Joseph Glanvil 1681)

Faerie tales, like folk customs, stimulate essential healing and coping mechanisms that transpose through culture providing by association, a means to remove our fear of the unknown, specifically those fears that manifest in dream and nightmare. Combative plot and structure enjoin a satisfying prophylactic that avers evil, allowing good to triumph. The 'good' is of course pre-determined and employs the same tricks and deceits as its opposition, albeit in the pursuit of perceived justice.

Faerie tales communicate best on a subliminal level through their subtle use of symbol, addressing generational rather than individual problems. Yet, it is only when factual knowledge is turned into personal knowledge that the individual may profit.[9] Set in liminal time, remote from 'conscious' reality, our fantasies and fears are purged in relative safety. When beating the Devil in 'faerie stories,' fear of him is subjugated in one reality, which is thereafter transmuted to another as a victory.

Children's chasing games also present and express a healthy fear of the supernatural, enacting the pursuit and torment by and the subsequent engagement with something 'other.' Enchantment becomes the vehicle for catharsis wherein poetic use is made of allegory and metaphor. Whether in folk-rhyme or ritual, we may face our irrationality; here we harmonise all disparate aspects of the psyche that together overwhelm the ego, the 'Devil' within, thus defeating the 'Devil' without. Though when this tool is removed, the ego runs free endorsing a self-serving and self-destructive Fate; such a dynamic can be seen as a pact with the 'Devil' at an inner level, being as 'real' as that perceived externally.

Exploring fantasies is clearly a healthy necessity. Both children and adults need recourse to alternative realities in order to redress the imbalance of an often single reality locked into the mind, which more properly 'exists' ubiquitously in all realities. Deprived of an outlet for this capacity to regain some measure of control, the mind suffers alienation, paranoia, cynicism and disintegration. Distinct from other grander narrative forms, these sentient folk traditions thrive on their own volition. More importantly, life's own experiences provoke recognition through the ensuing narrative, where a certain knowing induces contentment in the forthcoming happy ending. The 'Devil' can be bested, but only if we use our wits and cunning. This is the purpose of the 'burlesque' Devil in folk custom by whom we are redeemed only if the ability to change our self perception exists. Then medieval 'Grand Narratives' exploited this particular motif to great effect in numerous common works. The best of these explored the '*Nekyia*,' a classical theme of sorcery and the Underworld realm of shades in which either the hero embraces his quest for a new life that unfolds only during a series of challenging encounters with both death and the Devil, acknowledged jointly as the hand of Fate, or 'Providence.'[10] Moreover, to writers of the Middle Ages, the infernal world of 'faerie' was commensurate to the classical kingdom of Pluto and Proserpina: a context that influenced literary genres for several centuries to come.[11]

Indo-European burlesque folklore exhibits two types of narrative, one in which a compact between a person and the 'Devil' is forged and another where no compact exists. Both however, regularly pronounce defeat upon the outwitted 'Devil,' at least that is until the Reformation, when the Lutherans claimed the Devil could declaim mastery even without it.[12] Through the folktale medium we may trace the metamorphosis of the Devil from his role as trickster and buffoon, a social caricature whom one could enlist and then outwit, to infernal diabolist and triumphant stealer of souls, before finally resuming his semi-burlesque persona in post 18th century folk tradition. Though many classic folk examples of the compact survive nationally, this essay focuses primarily upon the region of Sussex as a tribute to several deceased members of Clan Tubal Cain, who either lived or worked at various magical and historical sites littered across its rolling chalky downs.

Additionally, in support of this, an abstract study of the Devil's distinctive role at large serves to reveal his innate *adversarial* force in a context that overshadows all localised and idiosyncratic variations of folk custom. In particular, the impact at popular level and perceived manifestations of the Devil are highlighted. In one generic collection of superstitions and folk customs, Roy Palmer discusses the 'challenge' where a known braggart, guilty of some form of hubris is pitted against the Devil in a game, a race, or exhibition of skill in various crafts from playing musical instruments to spinning.[13] Invariably, these reveal how, before and after the period of intolerance and paranoia (mainly accepted as taking place from the late 15th century through to the middle of the 17th century), the 'Devil' was summarily outwitted by the extra ordinary cunning of certain individuals! Bargains were struck, for fame, fortune, knowledge or power, with a Devil hard pressed to concede, or so the legends affirm.

Other tales relate to certain domains or areas where the Devil has particular power; one such genre conveys the curious potency of soil in the desolate, northern section of any graveyard. Held to be the province of the Devil, it is reserved for the reluctant burial of suicides, paupers, indigents and un-baptised folk. Here it is believed, he claims his own without recourse to trickery. In an extension of this belief the Devil even claims the first corpse buried in any new graveyard as an accepted tithe.[14] Likewise, the Devil allegedly claimed the first child baptised in any new church. Generally, that heinous entrance by which the Devil makes his escape when expelled by the baptismal cries of infants, was the Northern door; though many are now clearly disused and others bricked up. One north door in Pevensey (Sussex) has three crosses carved upon it to ward off the Devil; according to local folklore, he is believed even now, to lay in wait. If during a baptismal rite the baby did not cry, it was taken as a fateful indication of a short life.

A case, in 19th century rural Sussex records the reprimand by a grandmother to a child's nurse for not pinching it when it failed to cry.[15] Graveyard 'watchers' are those who upon being buried last, are assigned the post of guardian of the graveyard, ever ready to summon all those about to join it. It is a responsibility that expires upon the internment of the next corpse; cogently, the Devil though, was frequently credited with this duty in popular myth.[16]

So fearful too was the accepted wisdom in folklore that the Devil claimed his due in all covenants and compacts, complex burials were instigated to out manoeuvre him by laying the corpse to rest 'neither in nor out' (in the porch or wall), these being but two examples of the lengths people were prepared to go to avoid going to the Devil.[17] This is a revealing testament to the unrelenting and canny nature of humanity in the face of even the ultimate adversary, and of a hope that he could be defeated. It does of course emphasize something even more fascinating and self-serving - that of man's willingness to engage with the despised 'other,' in order to improve his lot.

The Devil was a powerful ally in the execution of this purpose, and if the advocate were clever enough, he would not even need to keep his half of the bargain. Favouring the magical and esoteric potency of the highly significant number seven or its multiples, many such bargains expose the Devil's handiwork, especially where impossible feats are set, such as the reaping of a whole field in a single night, or the building of bridges, or walls, even churches, all in exchange for a soul. Naturally, when the time came for the soul to be given up, the Devil was often cheated of his measure by some cunning device of an artful foe, commonly involving an animal being the first across the threshold, bridge or hearth.[18]

Before society ceased in its ability to laugh at itself, lingering beliefs frequently associated with dwindling Paganism, preserved overwhelming examples of folklore and custom that depicted the comedic Devil as a veritable simpleton, a ribald figure of ridicule, with names such as *'Lusty Dick,'* or the exceptionally curious *'Rumplestiltskin,'* proving more popular even than his growing reputation as the great 'trickster.'[19] This latter alliance is more generally a clerical preference, and refers more properly to his role as 'the ape of God;' the former has merit in its suggestion of the Nordic figure, Thor, whose antics and dull wits earned him an affectionate place in the hearts of the general populace.[20] Many variations of the 'compact' theme were given vent in the Legend of Faust, speculatively based on a very real 16th century German necromancer. Here, especially in Marlowe's version, we find again the comic figure of a burlesque Devil (*Mephistopheles*), who can be cheated if the exponent has sufficient wit. But, this Faust did not have that prerequisite and paid his due.

Nevertheless, Faust's crime was not in accepting his compact with the Devil but lay in his use of the Devil as an *adverse* magical force, to *oppose* faith with knowledge, to *oppose* abstinence with indulgence and tragically for him, to *oppose* Fate, which the clerics proclaimed belonged to God alone.[21] Instructions to break such compacts are supplied in the '*Magi Naturalis et Innaturalis*' and its many facsimiles.[22] Paracelsus, the successful alchemist and father of the science of medicine is also credited with having duped the Devil from his due by tricking him back into his incarceration as a spider within a hole in a tree.[23]

Adjunct to plays and other entertainments, festivals also sustain the theatre of illusion and evocatively trigger collective folk memory, inviting the interplay of certain enigmatic characters. One of these, the '*Herlekin*'[24] was a very dramatic but 'comedic' Devil with connections to the fey, the faerie folk, appropriately portrayed as a prince of faerie in the 13th century stage play – '*Jeu de la Feuillie*'.[25] At a popular level, the burlesque Devil and the 'fair folk' clearly belonged together in the enchanted realms. Such beliefs were the foundation of later associations with witchcraft. Indeed, his sly cunning was often compared to the wiles of womankind, and the Devil it seems was not averse to appearing as either a woman, or in the guise of one.

According to Jurich,[26] women (as naturally diabolical creatures) were often more likely to outsmart the Devil, paving the way for their later depiction as capricious harpies practising sinister acts of maleficarum, in preference to being the simple dupes of the Devil. Jurich[27] cites many European folktales in which the Devil is scared of the tricks and ploys of women. Often, powerful women who are able to subdue their lovers were said to have assumed the animal (totemic) power of the Devil. In spite of this obvious character flaw, the Devil is also a useful ally, a powerful protagonist, in fact a force invoked *adverse* to another. In this way, a negative neutralises or binds another negative. Baneful hemlock, denoted as a witch's plant, evocatively drawing its power from the 'Devil,' is put to use as a healing salve, where it is set in *opposition* to the disease. This belief reveals a spiritual level of healing in addition to that of the physical properties of the plant itself. Of course, the recipes do contain other narcotics and natural entheogens, having juice, seed and root concocted according to variable but once tightly guarded recipes.[28]

A certain procedure for self-empowerment through an invocatory compact with the Devil involves the complex extraction of the frog or toad bone. Charms of this nature vary across counties, but normally entail a gruesome and excruciating death for the unfortunate frog or toad, whose excarnated bones are disarticulated by throwing them into a stream at midnight, retrieving the one screaming bone that flowed contra to the others, upstream. This esteemed bone was endowed with similar powers to that carried by the 'Toadmen,' the infamous and enigmatic horse-masters, whose power drawn through this bone generated fear amongst the common folk, convinced its carrier must be in league with the Devil![29] An alternative rite requires that the bone, once won, be taken to a stable or a graveyard for three consecutive nights, whereupon the Devil, in order to preserve this power for himself, must attempt to wrest it from its claimant; to best him then, is to earn the right to carry it.[30] Russell asserts that:

> "neither theology nor history can prove the existence of the Devil, but they do reveal a belief in that existence, and subsequently their actions and reactions relative to it." [31]

Unsurprisingly then, the belief in and the perception of the Devil at a popular level, as reflected in the communal fears and fantasies prior to the persecutions was very different to the Devil of the clerics, who were ever inclined towards sorcery and maleficarum.[32] Interestingly, even here, the Church originally claimed that the power and force of the Devil utilised by witches from their compacts with him, was sanctioned by God! He was testing and routing out sinners for the Church to redeem or send to damnation. It would be some time yet before the Church would accept an independent Devil.[33] However, there existed no clerical dualism or heretical evils at the popular level, where the world was unequivocally populated with all manner of interactive and transitional ambivalent phenomena. By all accounts, Sussex was a county converted to Christianity later than many others (circa the 7th century), although it did embrace that faith emphatically thereafter, tenaciously maintaining a vestigial memory of Pagan beliefs and superstitions for many centuries after these things had been forgotten elsewhere.

Various names exist in Sussex for the Devil, some typical and generic, others not; these names suggest extreme respect and caution in their use – for to say his name was considered an actual evocation to manifestation! They range then, from the *'poor man,' 'old nick,' 'old scratch,' 'old man'* and even *'old grim,'* to the more informal and prosaic, Beelzebub and Puck, and then to the less respectful yet more indicative of the ridicule common to tales involving these two latter and most particular facets of this compound figure. Even where he is often the victim, the Devil is given his due respect; Devil's Dyke, is for example, referred to by locals as 'the poor man's wall.' Beelzebub remains an extant popular local variant within many Sussex Mummers Plays.

In the writings of Robert Cochrane, he mentions his belief that Shakespeare knew a thing or two about the old Craft.[34] Certainly, many of the plays attributed to Shakespeare do contain oblique references to folk customs and supernatural beliefs. Best known of these is the beautifully evocative, oneiric masterpiece, *A Midsummer Night's Dream*. Despite Shakespeare's portrayal of the faeries as uncharacteristically endearing for that period of history, they are nonetheless, quite skilled manipulators, distributing gifts or forfeits to those who aid or oppose them. They inflict acts of malice, use charms and seem thoroughly amoral. Within the enchanted realms the mundane obfuscations associated with witchcraft and faerie lore become blurred yet further, fuelling folk custom at the popular level.

Valiente shares with us her local knowledge of eccentric customs, particularly of the speculatory aboriginal race of small dark forest dwellers frequently associated with Ashdown Forest and Romany activity until well into the 19th century and whose 'clannish' behaviour (in the sense of closed families) was treated with much fear and suspicion.[35] Deep wisdoms are found embedded within the garbled superstitions of folkloric belief, and I would suggest the probability that the seven year sacrificial tithe to the 'otherworldly' realms refers more properly to the favoured magical number of the 'devil' and his 'faerie' mistress as agents of Fate, applied as a sacred term of office in the Suzerainty of kingships, priesthoods, heroic compacts and which are intrinsically linked to the natural regenerative growth cycles of mind (ego) in accord with matter (physical evolution).

As a descriptive term, 'faerie' is old French for enchantment, relating to ineffable and unquantifiable phenomena linked with this realm of the 'other,' where unknown and inexplicable forces were at play, but which invoked the presence of 'Fate.' The forms and perceived manifestations of these forces are fundamentally linked to culture and geography, transforming over time the adjective into a noun. Most notable are the dark and light elves of Alfheim (*Elphame*), drawn from the Norse corpus of belief, supplemented by a variety of pixies, goblins and boggarts which are also the rich legacy of 'Celtic' speaking confederates of Northern Europe.[36] Faerie lore is given tentative associations of racial or indeed ethnic memories regarding aboriginal ancestors, remote in time and who shared the deific and sentient forces of our natural and supernatural worlds.

These nature sprites are conceptually expressed as either aerial or chthonic, whose hypnogogic interactions are sought at liminal and interstitial times and locations. In other words, they are governed by strict laws, which have generated an abundance of superstition and taboo, attested historically throughout the British Isles beginning with those of the Roman obsession with the Lares, or ancestral agents of Fate. Interestingly, Valiente asserts how the best magic, utilised especially in cursing is that which invokes 'Fate' as the vengeful (ancestral) power for transgressions not settled by human law, revealing the use and assistance of the faerie denizens of the other world, either by compact, covenant or symbiosis.[37] Coterminous to this is the cognate form of the Devil *'teufel,'* a Germanic derivative meaning the opposer or opponent.[38]

A Roman altar, now in a Scottish library bears an inscription *'Dis campestribus,'* meaning gods of the countryside (locale), and is intriguingly remarked upon by a local guide as an inference to those that 'know' better - that these 'gods' are in fact faeries![39] Local tutelary Pagan deities were evidently woven into the telling and re-telling of these phenomena, increasing the superstitious awe attached to them, eventually becoming transposed to the expanding witchcraft acculturation of the Middle Ages during the term of social and religious paranoia. Hence, a mistress of a coven may be referred to as a queen, and the master, her partner as the 'devil' or better, the king of the 'Otherworld.' Favoured places for contact with denizens from these other realms are naturally those closest either to the sky and the Earth: hilltops, high ridges, etc and caves, or chambered tombs, etc, respectively. Obviously these areas have accumulated an immense body of phenomena related superstitions and magical kudos within folklore, custom and tradition. For the brave, or wise, these portals have provided contact and even alleged relationships between mortals and the 'fair folk' for many centuries.

By the 17th century, such activities were understandably demonised so that all spirit encounters were to be avoided rather than procured for fear of prosecution. This became problematic, especially for those who claimed either special gifts or powers from the faeries, or for those with faerie spouses (common even into the 19th century) leading to complex and secretive procedures. Provenance of such transmissions generated a mystique and glamour around anyone who professed to know of these matters. Authorities, self-proclaimed or otherwise were consulted for all manner of phenomena related incidents and were expected to give advice on how to interpret strange occurrences, to either ensure the blessings of the 'fair folk' or to lift a curse (harsh Fate) cast by them.

Oral authority, passed mouth to ear, prevented unwarranted dissemination of various local folk wisdoms. A precious association unprovable as a remnant from Roman occupation, now widely speculated upon is that of Diana as the Goddess of Fate whose wheel is turned by Lucifer. In other words, these monarchs of fortune, karma, change and progress, were simultaneously the fair folk, the witch king and queen, ancestral kin, and ancient god forms; once propitiated, but becoming increasingly feared or worse, abandoned.

A study of the names or euphemisms that alluded to this range of beings suggests the prevalence of these two major archetypes in popular belief. In Yorkshire and Derbyshire, the commonest name for the Devil was Hob or '*Old Hob*,' and is very possibly an acronym of '*Hob o' t'*

Hurst.' A curious domestic variant of this is d'obbie, compacted to serve his human host, and who is yet another example of the respectful symbiosis believed to exist between 'them' and 'us.' He has a counterpart known in Sussex as Master Dobbs, but in the Isle of Man, he carries the more enigmatic eponym *'fynoderee'* which means somewhat cogently, the 'hairy one.'[40] Described in like manner of Cain, he is wild, hirsute, short and ugly with oversized hands and feet. *'T'owd 'ob'* carries his huge holly club, ceaselessly roaming the dark and brooding landscape of the moors, taking respite in caves or in natural ridge fissures.[41] This fierce Anglo-Saxon spirit was assigned to the wild moors and was originally a *'thurse'* or *'thyrs,'* whose best known example found in the figure of Grendel is immortalised in the epic tale of Beowulf. [42]

This heroic narrative relates the mythological history of the Rhineland around the 6th century CE. Grendel, central to the plot, is the last of his kind and is here presented as a monstrous wight (similar to Norse ogres) or murderous giant. As the kin of Cain, he suffers, sharing his Fate, a derisory doom of banishment, contempt and brutality. Cain is said to be exiled within the Moon, now accompanied by those who follow him. His shadow reveals his burden, Abel, carried for seven hundred years before his burial beneath seven oak trees.[43] It is impossible now to determine just how much of all of this curious lore is a later Christian gloss when translated, and how much is true to the original account, but medieval audiences would have easily grasped its association.

Grendel is eventually killed for Cain's alleged sin of fratricide and for his kind's choosing to make war on God, a crime shared with the elves and other *'etins'* who are chillingly portrayed with all the guile and cunning of Cain.[44] This is a serious and perplexing departure from the usual genre that often represented such monsters as dull-witted imbeciles.[45]

When such archaic figures are encountered, especially *'Hob,'* a beautiful maiden may charm him; wit defeats him, but neglect, hubris or disrespect incurs his savage wrath. The challenge is there for all who feel themselves able to take him on and best him. Within all of this there is a sense of meted justice of some divine law invoked and put into play, the rules of which are understood and accepted by both parties, or *should* be. Traditional and Hereditary Craft especially asserts this knowledge and heeds it wisely. Furthermore, access to these otherworldly realms is said to impart its visitors with extraordinary gifts, an acknowledgement for their endeavours in the form of a mark, a shadow of these shining realms. This mantle, though much respected throughout the 18th and 19th centuries, was concealed during the earlier 16th and 17th centuries. The mentoring in these realms is recorded as adhering to sexual polarities, and reflects the male and female mysteries in particular of the Clan of Tubal Cain. Harte records several cases of various women whose testimonies reveal the mythology and psychology of such acts even during the period of intolerance in Great Britain generated by the Continental Inquisition.[46]

Descriptions of their faerie mentors are of a typically dark and brooding figure, more typical in fact of those that would be increasingly associated with the 'Devil,' especially after the Reformation. Supplementary to the over familiarised devil's dozen, the Devil traditionally favours seven or its multiples in all compacts and is the number oft quoted in relation to bargains struck with the 'fair' or 'good folk,' and also to experiences shared with them in alternate realities. The legends of Tam Lin, Thomas the Rhymer and Tannhauser recount this parallel feudal compact, typically a seven year allegiance after which a forfeit, often in the form of a tithe or *teind* is demanded.[47] The cycle may then be repeated.[48] Seven is also a number appreciated and honoured within many modern Craft practises, in particular, where matters of law and justice invoke and/or bind Fate. Reflected earnestly within the Clan of Tubal

Cain, this scion connects the Craft to the fey, where all initiates, including the Magister renew their oaths of Suzeraadd to the Maid, who through the Clan Egregore (which she holds as mistress of Fate) accepts all forfeits, and restores them and their shared Wyrd to the fold.[49] This commonality is no coincidence.

Enchantment thrives on belief rather than fact; reality is bound by perception. Therefore, inherited lore even where it devolves into superstition (that is a law or taboo no longer properly understood) is instinctively acknowledged and given consideration. The magic manifests through illusion; it matters not whether the reality of it is in the mind or of matter. If it has worked on whatever level, then it is deemed to be a success. And this is precisely where the power of place adds to that effect, affecting the mind on many levels. It is first disarmed by the suggestion of phenomena related to its locale then it becomes suggestive to any natural elemental activity before finally succumbing to supernatural activity, real or perceived.

Therefore, if we are told that running round a particular gravestone 49 times at cockcrow will evoke the shade of its departed owner, from whom we may ask a boon if bribed sufficiently with whisky and tobacco, then we will perform this activity with all surety that it will succeed. Moreover, our apprehension will effect an experience of confirmation. Imagine then, how much more potent such suggestions would have been to our great, great, great grandparents, who suffered not the malaise of modern cynicism. This is why, though many of these concepts remain within Traditional Craft, they are generally awarded little more than lip service; sadly, continuity rarely equates with comprehension.

The rules of engagement are strict and precise and have all been probable precursors for many magical practices in ritual. Hand gestures, the use of symbols, incantations and favoured correspondences are culturally conditioned enactments of taboos and propitiatory superstitions when evoking the presence of otherworld denizens. As our tolerances for their amorality increased, so did the ways in which we chose to conceive of them as purely either good or bad. Here, the paraphernalia and procedures for engagement became ever more elaborate. Keep it simple I was told. Good advice: remove the cynical and ignorant abuse of form and revert to a respectful appreciation and acceptance in ambivalence for its own sake. Once this is understood, real magic can be truly apprehended.

Household items that have been processed such as bread, iron, salt, fire and even flax, were commonly incorporated into spells and charms by cunning-folk to counter the power of the faerie, who it was supposed would shrink from these civilising amenities. In centuries past, everything had an approachable and familiar form, however grotesque or bizarre, and force was never perceived as a nebulous or transcendental quality. Quite simply, if a thing could be known, it could be defeated. In this context it becomes easier to grasp the mettle of eccentricity with regard to effecting magic. Folktales, customs and superstitions were all reliant upon a coded allusion to both form and force and were subversive in intent towards the many by the few. Knowledge has always been power; the difficulties in keeping one's family safe from all manner of beings from this world or another meant an imposition of boundaries and taboo. Breaking those was a risky business, entered into under extreme duress or in times of great need, or, with an alternative understanding by those in the '*know*.' Fate hovers on the edge, of consciousness, of time and of space. The rational becomes irrational to gain experience of its purpose, hence the apparent nonsense associated with many charms, spells and rites of divination… '*he who dares, wins,*' a better maxim for magic than war.

Fate as the hand of 'Providence' manifested as varying degrees of caprice across the length and breadth of these enchanted isles. The more prosperous the area, the more kindly the faerie benefactors; where deprivation and harsh poverty ensued, the more inclined to spite the 'fair folk' became. Yates recounted his otherworld experiences and remained convinced that the faerie folk are here to 'teach us in accord with Fate,' when at the *'reathes of the year,'* the marked pathways were open to brave seekers.[50] The pattern is clear. In folk custom, spells and formulae exist for contacting the otherworldly realms and for gaining knowledge at the behest of both the faerie queen and her consort, the Devil. When aid is required, he can be summoned unrestrictedly into this realm, but she may ride out only on the reathes. He is the tempter and trickster who may yet be outwitted if sufficient guile is employed. Whitlock cites the power of the Devil as an amalgamation of archaic forces and adversarial traits, which if summoned correctly will serve, if not, then the penance was believed to be swift, brutal and quite terrible.[51] Even so, many folk tales do reveal many successful instances where the Devil was outwitted by cunning or superior action.

On Highdown Hill near Worthing, stands a folly known as the Miller's Tomb where a seven circuit run and chant will summon the Devil, in the local form of the 'Miller,' a name used by Evan John Jones in referring to the presence of this enigmatic figure, particularly at another local site upon which he worked and one reputedly worked by other Sussex covens in years past.[52] Friday is given as a good day for making bargains or exacting challenges, generally explained as the accepted day of Christ's crucifixion, though Roy Palmer suggests an interesting alternative - with Friday being the day that Adam and Eve were expelled from Eden, making an older link with more archaic ante-deluvian forces and mythical Cainite ancestry.[53]

Superstitious fishermen, would not at one time put to sea on a Friday, this being '*Tip T'od's*' day![54] Another tale from Arundel in Sussex recalls the fall of the prideful Devil, hurled from Heaven into the bramble thicket by St. Michael, thereafter celebrated according to the Julian calendar on old Michaelmas. Weaving a clever graft, Pagan and Christian folklore asserts a synthesis that would develop into the dual faith practice of many Cunning Folk. Another tradition rationalises how the Devil in order to keep control of his many servants through their compacts with him, does not give the witch the power to place and lift a hex; generally, she may place them, but a cunning man or woman, having more wit to strike a better bargain, is better able to do both.[55]

A keen folklorist, Doreen Valiente collated many fascinating tales and customs, some of which she discusses at length within her numerous books and articles.[56] She suggests how the '*oscalum infame,*' a grave charge once levied against the Templars, heretics and many later witches was in fact a burlesque of irreverent buffoonery, nothing more than a theatrical gesture of mock contempt – "*kiss my arse,*" oft and ignorantly repeated to this day! But Muchembled confirms this once serious act of obeisance more properly confirms a more specific relationship that assigns absolute *fealty*; a not insignificant factor in the alleged compact between the Devil and his postulant.[57] In another tale, Kent gifted to its county a rich legacy in its many Midwinter customs and celebrations that honour and revere the horse, the Earth and solar light. Modern Mummers plays despite their mercenary intent retain vestiges of folk custom in the archetypes chosen in the cast.

Primary of these is the burlesque Devil who as Beelzebub, wields both club and tramp's stick, possibly another symbol of and allusion to the nomadic wanderer, an exile, a stark reminder of latent power, a trickster still, should anyone come forward to meet his challenge.[57] Valiente refers to witchcraft as a: *'religion of the dispossessed and the outlawed'* in essence as unsettled as the Romany folk she describes and whose main deity speculated as *'Tubalo,'* is referred to simply as *'Deval'* or *'Duval,'* again paralleling that of the coven master, particularly in the sense of an embodiment of Virtue.[59] Virtue held by the Devil or Magister encompasses an initiate into a Clan family with his protection. Scottish trial records of 1699 relate how the hands of the Devil would be placed, one on the head of an initiate, the other under the soles of their feet so that *'all between them'* would be pledged in total *surrender* to him! This was *not* a passing of any power, but an act of Suzerainty over the initiate.[60]

What this reveals is the abject belief in the compact during this period, the fealty and the absolute power of the Magister as the devil's representative. Yet even this was reciprocal, as the Devil in return was obliged to teach and protect his initiates. In Sufism, the Devil is described as the 'tempter, yet teacher,' an appreciation of not only his ambiguity but of his primal role as 'agent provocateur' in the dark theology of our evolution.[61] The context had shifted due to diabolism, but the folk custom remained intact. This is a recognised motif whereby the person who serves becomes intrinsically bound to their liberator, in this case – the 'Devil,' and when the candidate also receives their 'mark' of both homage and vassalage. Many branches of Traditional Craft uphold this principle, and the late Robert Cochrane in particular claimed this title in his role as Magister of Clan Tubal Cain; nonetheless, he reiterated recognition of a 'higher' authority than his own.[62]

Traditional knowledge was often passed in secret fraternities. One of these was the society of horsemen, a rural organisation that fiercely protected its lore. All teachings were customarily oral, from mouth to ear; records were forbidden, all had to be remembered by initiates into these groups. But it was often sound advice and practise; appearing as magic or 'arcane gibberish' only to those who were not in the 'know.' Of course, a certain flair and aptitude was essential, just as with any Craft, and this elusive ingredient could not be taught. Initiates were given a 'word' of power, allegedly their guard against the Devil, whose word it was, even as they wielded its power.

According to legend, the first horseman was reputed to be Cain forging yet another link between this agricultural figure and the Devil. Given that Cochrane's father was allegedly a 'horsemen,' this may possibly have influenced his choice of name for his Clan. Another notorious cunning-man active during the latter half of the 19th century was George Pickinghill. Rumoured to have been a renowned 'horse whisperer,' Pickinghill allegedly held one of his several Cuveens in rural Sussex. He claimed to have enigmatically predicted the revival in 1962 of the 'Old Craft.'[63] Coincidently, Prof. Hutton makes the observation that Robert Cochrane possibly released his first published work in that very year: 1962. Clearly this was a fateful and auspicious date in the historiography of the Craft.[64]

Diverse communal customs and rites of passage immersed the farm labourer within the superstitions and lore that saturated traditional rural practices. Cogently, the leader or foreman drawn from among the harvesters was known as the 'Lord' or 'Drighton' in Anglo-Saxon terminology, to whom his men 'owed reciprocal duty.' All newcomers were initiated according to medieval custom wearing a 'halter' submitting their oaths to this 'Lord' and his 'Lady.'[65] He was the surrogate 'Master' for the Manorial, (or feudal Lord) and one of his obligations was to ensure the provision of vitals and all *good fayre* for his men. As host in this sense, he is perceived by some as having parallels with the faerie 'lords' and with the greenwood lord, Robin Hood.[66]

These patterns suggest the template for many later 'Craft' traditions, and the scion between the feudal compact, the superstitious reverences and the mentoring system, often secret, can be evinced within them. One of these events, bound intrinsically to Martinmas is held in honour of the patron Saint of smiths and labourers and was the traditional time for the agricultural hiring fair. A huge feast of bread, cheese and whiskey, or more generally ale, both welcomed the new labour and celebrated for the last time the camaraderie with those leaving. All manner of labour including ploughmen and carters were contracted to prepare the fields and animals for winter. One custom peculiar to this fair, was that *'blood should be spilt on this day to secure good fortune for the next twelve months,'* referring of course to the necessary annual slaughter of livestock for the winter.[67]

Even when celebrated at a domestic level, an ox or a fowl at least was duly prepared and mindfully consumed. It was a celebrated public holiday and one of the few days in rural employment where no work was undertaken. Initiations into Horsemen's Societies normally took place on this auspicious eve and the barn was often a favoured location. Three knocks upon the door and the declaration that the candidate was there at the behest of the Devil gained them admittance to the smell of burning sulphur. Led in, under the Moon, blindfolded he would then be enjoined to take *'a shak o' ould hornie,'* the hand of the Devil over which the pledge or covenant was declared:

> 'to hele, concele and ne'r reveal; neither write, nor dite,
> nor recite; nor cut, nor carve, nor write in sand.'

The hand of the Devil was of course that of the Master Horsemen, who, wearing a horned mask was draped in a calf skin speculatively rubbed with phosphorous. The pledge bound them never to reveal the horsemen's 'word' (of power), to anyone who wore an apron except a smith or farrier. Smiths were also held in awe, wielding the power to heal and *expel* baneful influences. The ceremonial toast was to Cain, as the first master of the art:

'Here's to the horse with the four white feet,

The chestnut tail and mane,

A star on his face and a spot on his breast,

And his master's name was Cain.'

According to folklore, they were shown the ritual handshake in order to greet and recognize a true 'brother' and taught many charms; some were reputed to invoke the assistance of the Devil himself by right of the toad bone.[68] The Devil as a master craftsman was also allegedly a smith whose civilizing arts repelled the darkness and ignorance of tribal societies. Though not all engagements were beneficial, especially those that challenged Fate; the best example of this, is gambling. Playing cards were typically referred to as the devil's books, not because they were evil per se, but because they engaged Fate to manipulate the outcome. Perceived as hubris to challenge the Devil at his own game, the odds were never good.

Adversarial battles between the old Pagan gods and the encroaching influences of Christianity are speculated within folklore to account for many of the topographical anomalies across the British Isles. Many hills and mounds especially (abode of faerie in folk tradition) are littered with huge boulders, said to be the abandoned load of the Devil in hasty retreat of some cunning peasant's quick action. One well-known hill on the Sussex Downs is named '*Old Harry*' after one of the local names for the Devil enigmatically referred to by locals as the 'provider.' Not in the Christian sense of 'Providence,' for this current of Fate has primal undertones and is even the subject of a dedicatory prayer within the Wicca of Gerald B Gardner. Again this is redolent of Woden (*Nikker*) and Pwca, both deific spirits of the wild and inexplicable realms of enchantment.[69]

Another hill on the Downs, noted for similar associations is *'Thundersbarrow Hill'*, dedicated to Thunor (*Thor*). Nearby is 'Puck's Croft', revealing the folk belief in the pervading sense of the 'other' in and around these areas of topographical enchantment.[70] Rudyard Kipling while living in Sussex wrote the highly inspirational and evocative 'Puck of Pook's Hill' in 1906, influencing much of the 20th century paganism. Geoffrey Ashe noted how on some but not all levels, the druidic passion for triads is shared by faerie lore and how they both revere the fundamentally similar ancient high palaces and secret groves, albeit the former is a solar belief system and the latter is presented as lunar.[71]

Even so, dancing in circles, the use of the number three, or multiples of it, and the reverence for the sidhe or sacred mounds, indicates an accrued synthesis in some revivalist Craft and neo-pagan practices, formerly at the popular level at least since the 18th century. To place these beliefs in context, during the latter part of the 17th century, over 3 million predictive Almanacs were sold, more even than the Bible! Containing information on astrology, festivals, prophecies, tides, eclipses et cetera; that were mainly of use to fishermen, farmers and other agricultural workers. Superstition and custom were the datum by which their lives were scheduled.[72] One of the oldest known published incantations professed to summon the Devil is the *'Bagabi Rune'* from a 13th century play by the minstrel, Ruteboeuf.[73]

In Traditional Craft and folk custom, to 'whistle up' the Devil is generally to brew up a storm – another connection to Thor perhaps? Churches too are places where the Devil may be summoned by running around the grounds at midnight. But again, this may be a garbled re-telling of lore associated with the graveyard 'watcher.' Chanctonbury Ring is perhaps the most famous of all hills within the Sussex region. This is another place where an eerie atmosphere unnerves all those brave enough to summon the Devil on Midsummer's Eve, achieved by running backwards seven times around the summit at midnight. Should he appear, the request must be given before he has the chance to offer food in the form of meat broth or porridge, which the Summoner is obliged to consume and for which he takes their soul as payment.[74]

Few indeed would have the presence of mind to be so bold, or to remain calm enough to speak without delay, quelling all fear and wonder at such an occurrence. Hence arose the belief in the pre-requisite wit and cunning to accomplish such an ordeal and especially to live to tell the tale. In line with considerable local folklore regarding this and many other hills and mounds throughout Sussex, one tale, dated from the 1960s, preserves the enduring myth of faerie in the sighting of a fair lady poised elegantly upon her white horse.[75] Valiente claims to have worked at this notorious location with the oldest coven in the county during the early 1960s, adding that she was of the opinion it had been so used for centuries.[76]

Valiente worked here again a few years later with the Clan of Tubal Cain and at another location in Sussex, one very memorable 'All Hallow's Eve' is passionately recorded by her.[77] Devil's Dyke, a great cleft in the South Downs is according to local custom the means by which the Devil tried to drown the good people of Sussex in spite for their conversion to Christianity. But in this return to the burlesque he was thwarted by the quick wit of a local woman who it is said ran up the hill with a blazing lamp held behind a sieve, which confused the Devil and a cockerel, who, convinced it was dawn, began to crow; upon hearing this, the Devil absconded in great haste.[78] Donning feminine guise the Devil endeavoured to distract and waylay St Dunstan, a Saxon Archbishop of Canterbury in the 11ᵗʰ century from his toil in the smithy. Recognising the Devil by his cloven hooves peeping beneath his skirts St Dunstan saw him off with the red hot pincers on the end of his nose. He fled screaming and legend has it that he quenched his burning proboscis in the nearby springs of Tunbridge wells, which is a red and sulphurous brew even today.[79]

Other tales popular even in the early 20ᵗʰ century, relate several battles between the Devil and St Dunstan, that reveal him being bested by the cunning of the Saint, who used iron against his apparently faerie foe. The best of these describes a bargain struck between them, whereby the Devil was to leave all houses standing that sported a horseshoe over the door, as St Dunstan then hurtled at great speed to forge and hang them, ahead of the Devil. Beneath these quaint tales of buffoonery is juxtaposed the real fear of an otherworldly adversary, yet one that can be bested, either by wit or counter belief. In either case the Devil is the catalyst and empowering force for change or banishment of something unwanted or even baneful.

In the late 19ᵗʰ century, published reports about Sussex County included a tale about a Cunning-Man and his son from Crowborough who found themselves in trouble with the Devil, having temporarily forgotten the spell to dismiss him. Employing distraction to delay him, the son, scattered seeds upon the ground, instructing the Devil to pick them up, one-by-one; this clearly demonstrates the belief even as late as this that the Devil could be summoned and bound in service by those with the knowledge to do so. However, should that knowledge fail, then the situation was reversed. At the same time, faeries, or *farises'* in local parlance, were said to occupy a cavern at Beeding Hill, and the farmers especially remained on good terms with them; they believed that their presence brought prosperity to the farm, slights to them would bring ruin.[80] Cunning Murrell, from Essex, similarly declaimed himself – the 'devil's master.' Nevertheless, upon his death, many local folk expected the Devil to claim his own.[81]

Tradition asserts that the knowledge and authority to summon and make bargains with the Devil and the 'good folk' was passed from one to another through possession of the inherited 'familiar' spirit; said to be lodged *within* the body, this is evidently not a physical familiar. Only then can the former owner of this enigmatic personal Virtue die peacefully or abdicate these tied responsibilities where necessary, freed from the accrued 'karma' such an inherited compact carries. This is in essence the empowered and embodied force imbued by the Devil which should be given up at death in order for him to claim that soul. However, if such a force is 'passed on' then he is still bound to serve its living host. Another tale confirms belief in the receipt of this personal Virtue, from mother to daughter belying the refutation of same sex transmission.[82]

This 'Virtue' may also be ceded in artefacts, books and through the breath or repetition of certain words.[83] In Clanships, authority remains bound to these artefacts and the Clan Egregore, or group soul/mind, having a distinct purpose, is transmitted differently. Women as 'witches' have been perceived as having the ability to draw upon the power of the Devil directly through their sex, whereas men are required to summon or assume this force, hence the (general) gender distinction between 'witches' and 'cunning-men' (naturally this distinction did not apply to cunning-women, although they may have claimed a different source for their abilities). Intriguingly, for this reason, within the Clan of Tubal Cain, the Magister hold his office through the Maid he serves in his capacity as 'Devil.'[84]

Modern academia studying the historiography of the Craft now considers the valid distinction between belief and fact. Belief is what sustained the traditional practises of charmers, conjurors, cunning-folk and witches at the popular level where ordinary folk were subject to exploitation and abuse; but these Crafts also generated vital community, and pragmatic assurances against inexplicable and incomprehensible forces discernable even up to the onset of the Second World War. All of these claimed supernatural aid, be that from the Devil or the 'good folk.'[85] Robert Cochrane refers wistfully to the '*Faith*' as his Craft, and allegedly of five generations before him. Belief is a prime mover. *Faith* can and does move mountains.[86] Magic creates change through illusion. To say these things are not possible is to miss the point. Superstition naturally thrived on this premise, affording both the genuine and the unscrupulous equal means.

A Victorian cunning-man by the name of 'Pig-tail Bridger' from Sussex, was one of many across the country, renowned for claiming to be the 'devil's master.' These men were said to exude, command and to project 'glamour,' a clever personality tool to induce 'belief.'[87] Nevertheless, it is important to remember how these people were known as the natural enemies of the witch, so therefore when they were conjuring the 'Devil,' they did so to *combat* maleficarum, or so they claimed. In truth, they were more than capable of inflicting the same. But it is interesting to note the use of the devil's powers to combat negative acts, used in his *adversarial* capacity. His knowledge and power were drawn forth *against* other magics. Covenanted words, gestures and symbols ensured his recognition of the practitioner as a commanding force, held in a familial *compact*.

Cleverly, in order to avoid charges of heresy, though the Devil was clearly and unambiguously evoked, he was called forth under the authority of the trinity, whose *higher* status had to be acknowledged; this, witches would not do, believing their 'devil' to be the highest source. Even so, the adversary was employed by cunning-folk to solve the problem, to work *against* the thieves, to *ward* off malefic intent, and to *repel* a disease or affliction.[88] This could indicate a belief in the Christian Devil, as some believe, but it could also just as easily reveal a belief in a more complex figure, overlaid and enriched from diverse sources. All assert an ambivalent amoral force, capable of punishment or reward that submits to and respects superior wit, yet equally holds in contempt the weak for their hubris.

This description is surely more wide-ranging than that proffered by scriptorial dogma: Semantics or *'Faith'*? The choice is incumbent upon experience, always subjective and ever changing. How we perceive this adverse force determines our mastery of it, ergo, our rewards and achievements, as every good faerie tale reveals.

Robert Cochrane: 'The Faith of the Wise': The Man; the Myth and his Magic

This essay addresses the magical argosy of a man over whom much discourse has been aired and much ink spilled. In particular, his beliefs are frequently surmised through considered analysis of his letters. Naturally, few though they are in number, the letters are indeed a rich resource, yielding many insights, and yet paradoxically they merely shadow the more obvious pattern and development of the quite painful journey of self-realisation offered elsewhere. However, to discover this, we have to follow the pattern of his life and the influences brought to bear upon that discernable point.

The first priority is to here stress the most important factor that Robert Cochrane is first and foremost to those of his Clan, a revered ancestor for we are in fact, a Cult of the Ancestors and *not* a Cult of the Personality. So his personal life will not be discussed nor elaborated upon beyond what is unavoidable. Such matters are necessarily the concern of his extant family to whom we should all consider when highlighting his esoteric works. For context only, exploration then begins with the man. For those intrigued by matters more personal, numerous books and articles provide descriptive accounts of his life and death, presented sympathetically by the following authors:

Rebirth of Witchcraft by Doreen Valiente

Sacred Mask, Sacred Dance by E.J. Jones.
Western Traditions of Magic by William Gray
Witchcraft a Tradition Renewed by E.J. Jones
Gavin Semple for the Poisoned Chalice
and Mike Howard for numerous works.

The Man:

Born to [alleged] poverty in the slums of London on the 26th January 1931, Roy Leonard Bowers was one of eight children. He died, aged just 35 on the 3rd July 1966 leaving a flurry of unresolved controversy, an enigmatic legacy and a vibrant, evolving impact upon the Craft. In his short but anguished life, Robert Cochrane produced several works and numerous letters of which a mere handful have survived. These have captivated the occult scene for over 4 decades. His influence has been tremendous, stimulating the instigation of many new traditions and accelerating the evolution of others. Where based on his published letters, they are distinguished from his own hereditary lineage of the Clan of Tubal Cain by their generic Craft title of 'Cochranite.' Some of the major traditions founded on the premise of his works through people who knew and/or worked with him include Joe Wilson's '1734' tradition, Ruth Wyn Owen's 'Y Plant Bran,' Ronald 'Chalky' White and George Winter's 'Regency'; countless others remain anonymous to date.

Many lines of debate are fuelled by diverse views and opinions of both his life and work exist within the public remit. But the view expressed here is my own based on the tradition of his Clan, dedicated to its tutelary deity, named by him as Tubal Cain, god of smith craft, gnosis and evolution. Cochrane was an angry but passionate man, said to be violent, an anarchist in fact, yet also a deeply troubled individual much given to melancholia. Others record him as arrogant and ego-centric, blunt, a ranter and consummate trickster. Yet he would not deny any of these. He also declared that marriage had saved him from himself. His troubled spirit generated a certain 'wanderlust,' which enabled him access to what was at that time, obscure and remote pockets of fading rural traditions. Primarily, travel brought to him the traditional skills of smith craft, and introduced him briefly to life with the canal and barge folk before he finally settled in Slough where he lived and worked for seven years as a typesetter. During those crucial years he drew upon many influences including those from the small occult community who gravitated toward this striking figure. Of these, the best known were Ronald White and George Winter, referred to by those closest to them as 'Chalky and George.' These were later followed by Bill Gray, Evan John Jones, Norman Gills and Doreen Valiente. Although Doreen Valiente joined the Clan late in 1964, she stayed barely a year, leaving in 1965. She recorded her frustrations freely, but also her nostalgia and deep affection for Robert Cochrane. Within her note books, she describes in detail an ivory wand and carved cup that Robert Cochrane admired and sought to borrow. He also set her the task of making enquiries as to the price of a skull. This reveals that he very clearly did not have either in his possession at that time, affirming a fledgling group that had not quite formulated the variant strands of influence into a cohesive Mythos, nor yet acquired all the tools necessary for execution of its praxes.

His vision needed form. Reaching out through the media, Robert Cochrane attempted to manipulate the occult scene which he viewed as stagnant. Aiming pointedly at Wicca, he penned several articles which he envisaged would counter what he considered its detrimental and misleading influences. These were published as follows:

- *Psychic News* - Nov 63 – 'Genuine Witchcraft Defended'

[In this he presents an alternative 'hereditary' perspective of the Craft]

- *New Dimensions* - Nov 64 - 'Witches Esbat'

[Here he gives an account of a traditional cave rite]

- *Pentagram* Nov – 64 - 'The Craft Today'

[This is a rant against the prevailing media view of Craft as presented by those who followed Gerald B. Gardner]

- March 65 – 'On Cords'

[Magical uses for cords, knots and bindings]

- Nov 65 – 'Faith of the Wise'

[A mystical treatise asserting the Craft as a Mystery Cult]

The *Pentagram* had been produced by the 'Witchcraft Research Association.' Its publisher, Gerard Noel was also present as a guest at some of Robert Cochrane's workings much to the chagrin of Clan members of 'Full Admission.' In fact, this was to be a recurring issue between Robert Cochrane and his Clan members who were uncomfortable with the presence of non-'initiates.' Several contentious articles were composed by a curious fellow and associate of Cochrane's. Together they achieved considerable notoriety that led eventually [allegedly] to the magazine's closure. Taliesin referred to Cochrane as the *'Kier Hardie'* of the Craft and this succinct epithet best exemplifies Cochrane's mission and vision. His intention was nothing short of reform and consolidation under the auspices of his perception of Craft expression. An occult association was planned, executed through a 'Pagan Dawn' style network. This was obviously never realised.

Advertisements for contacts inspired a young Joe Wilson to respond in late 65. Some half-dozen letters traversed the 'pond' sourcing a myriad speculations and interpretations on their puzzling content. But it is important to remember, that when analyzing the writings of an author, the purpose and construction between a private letter and an article is of necessity very different. A letter, even where composed as an instructional missive is written to exchange personal information relevant to writer and recipient alone. Letters are written with singular significance, engineered around a matter of private import. An article issues a public statement, declaring or promoting a lecture of purpose to the masses.

Beyond its intimate parameter a letter loses its impact dramatically. Whereas an article is contrived to express one's beliefs quite specifically, honing in on points that emphasis ideas the author wishes the *public* to understand. Articles convey those thoughts we wish disseminated, those points of influence by which the aims drawn up at their commencement may be revealed unequivocally. For example a 'Manifesto' determines the aims, views and purpose of the person/s or party that releases it; private letters between those members and others will tend to reveal more about the personality of the individual.

Therefore, in conclusion of that premise, we would suggest contemplation and study of Robert Cochrane's articles in preference to his letters if his message is to be successfully deciphered and apprehended. If on the other hand, the man himself, his tricks, blinds and baffle captivate your imagination, then the letters provide this in abundance. Together of course, they reveal the man and his work, a most tantalizing combination. The Robert Graves letters (presented in appendix one of volume one) offer a rare opportunity to study unknown material. Sadly, very little more about the man or his beliefs is revealed, especially as they were written before Cochrane had fully formulated or correlated his ideas together. Here he is still testing the waters, still almost naive in his angst, still determined to assert himself in the face of what he considered to be a hostile world. His opinions are clearly disparate, confused in places and contradictory in others. They do not present his thoughts constructively. More useful to us are his articles, to which we shall return shortly, after we have explored the man and his myth in just a little more depth.

Within his letters to Bill (William) Gray written during 1964, he mentions consideration given to the formation of a second group, dedicated to a transcendent god, one not of the Sun or fields of Nature. Poetically, he describes the transcendent spirit of man as the unknown god. He shifts tack a few times but interspaces generalities with gems, small kernels of wisdom such as his advocation of balance as requisite, declaring the premise that nature abhors a vacuum; what we take out, must be put back. The aim here is to impress Bill that he understands the symbiotic relationship of the micro/macrocosm, wherein the shift of one's Fate by a Magus or Mystic, requires an equilibrating dynamic to stabilize the focussed actuation of the 'Work.'

Placing the virtue of Divine Love or Truth as paramount within his expression of the 'Faith,' he warns the pilgrim that only through pain and sheer force of will, such profound insights should prevail. The lesson is hard, he postulates, the reward inestimable, yet to grasp the reality that this Divine attribute is in fact ambivalent, is to break the heart of the devotee – but if man, preferring illusion, opposes Truth, then grief will follow. It is often declared, and by numerous others that Robert Cochrane was influenced by numerous books, including the inspired yet much criticised book: *The White Goddess* by Robert Graves of whom he declared himself, an "admirer and critic." Within the afore mentioned brief correspondence, Robert Graves advised Cochrane to:

"restore their original hunger for wisdom"

In this he achieved unmitigated success!

Myth:

Moving into a more contentious area, albeit the facet that is the most alluring, some may balk at the claim that Cochrane was heir to five known hereditary generations within the English Craft Traditions, but such things must be accepted as un-provable either way; for or against. The truth is here less important than the idea of it which spawned the myth; for it is the myth that generates the truth of the work. A paradox of the ilk much beloved of Cochrane and all aligned to that star. He announced that his Great Grandfather had been the Grand Master of the Staffordshire Witches that breached the Warwickshire border.

His Mother, he declared had been a Maid and scryer for an 'Old Cuveen' in Windsor.[89] As for his Father, the jewel in the crown resided in his profession as a Horseman. Religious conversion caused his Great Grandfather to curse the family for resorting to Methodism, for which act, it was claimed, sourced all Cochrane's ill luck. Nevertheless, after the death of his Father, his Aunt Lucy reputedly taught him the 'Arts of his Craft' through which he re-affirmed his birthright. Thereafter he described himself as a *'Member of the People, of the Clan of Tubal Cain.'* He was also given to referring to other terms and qualifications including: a pellar, a horseman, and the ladies were known as the green gowns, all the time being careful to stress that they were known only to *others* as witches. For himself, he specifically avoided that term, finding it self-limiting and even pejorative.

Romantically, he declared himself to be a dedicated follower, a man of 'Od.' Significantly, E. J. Jones also referred to his own similar assignment. Cochrane admitted to Bill Gray in a letter that the binding and absorption of spirits was not his field of expertise, or his real concern. Using idiosyncratic symbology he stressed pertinent aspects of the Clan's Mythos as paralleling the mystical elements of the Kabbalah - Bill's own field of expertise. According to his own teachings, Cochrane remained adamant that there are no real 'secrets' as everything is known and understood already by those who are true to their calling – To those who are not, then ego will blind them, shielding the beauty from the words exposed to them. But he did assert and adhere to the concept of 'sacred.' Certain things therefore were not discussed by him, his co-workers. In deference to this observation, neither shall we.

The Mysteries may only be revealed through experience; in fact they are inexpressible even after that. Words spoken or written concerning how these things may be achieved are merely instructions, vacuous information and totally useless in the hands of all but the true seeker who alone will properly identify through discernment and intuition the keys within them. According to traditional teachings regarding the Mysteries, anyone who professes to either 'withhold' admission to the Mysteries or who declare them to be dangerous to those whom they consider 'ill-prepared'; or who seek control of their dissemination within oath bound secrecy, are already lost to the realms of ego and will experience only the illusion it feeds on. A late letter to Joe Wilson spoke out against secrecy, advising him that wisdom is free to all who achieve it by their own merit - the Mystery should never be confused with the procedure used to obtain it. Information is just that! Without genuine experience, the Mystery remains veiled. These and other matters were his core principles upon which his Tradition and Mythos were founded.

Doreen Valiente further records that after his death, Robert Cochrane's widow told her he'd made it all up! Is this true we have to ask? But we can never really know. It is though, unlikely and predominantly unimportant. His work stands on its own, unparalleled and without precedent in this century. It bears no resemblance to any distinctly Wiccan based alternative, a factor that continues to fascinate many within and without Traditional branches of the Craft. Many therefore hail him as a genius, of singular charisma fuelled by something 'other.' This is verified by all those who worked with him, either by chance or design. His fire has been likened to that of an avatar, genii; or other psychopompic individual destined to lead and inspire true seekers to a realisation of gnosis within their own particular stream. To that end he implemented the 'Law' – this has now become his credo:

> "Do not what you desire – do what is necessary.
> Take all you are given – give all of yourself.
> What I have I hold.
> When all else is lost – and not until then.
> Prepare to die with dignity."

Rumours even now persist surrounding both his life and tragic death with a shroud of intrigue - of ritual sacrifice; but in death, speculation has merely escalated this role within the divine king cycle. The truth as ever, is much less sensational. Between the Winter Solstice of 1965 and the Summer Solstice of 1966, his final letters to Joe Wilson and Norman Gills embrace his desolation and sense of despair, particularly after his wife left him with their son in April of that year. Maudlin and depressed, he poignantly speaks of being without hope and of his epiphany, of spiritual strength coming from such adversity.

On Midsummer's Eve (June 23rd) he ingested poison, a deadly cocktail of Librium, hellebore and belladonna. To avoid any misunderstanding he left a lucid suicide note declaring himself of sound mind. Just a few days previously he'd visited E. J. Jones and his wife, jokingly stating that he would soon be hunting from the 'other' side. Thwarted even here, Fate held him back for nine more days; he was to die in hospital of a drug induced coma. His seven year term as Clan Magister further fuelled the belief in a sacrificial death.

Craft:

The pursuit of suitable ritual sites allowed Cochrane to indulge his passion for caving where his strong affinity with chthonic forces convinced him of the imperative for objective contact with these primal elements. Working outdoors as a robed Cuveen; the Clan moved around various sites across the South of England, including Burnham Beeches, Sussex Downs, Cheddar Gorge and Brecon Beacons. Described by some as 'shamanistic,' a term that was ironically, anathema to Cochrane, a technique he told Bill Gray was too primitive, he developed a freer more flamboyant style of expression, fuelled by spirit contact and the down load of inspiration received from it. He rejected the use of scripts as obstructive. Eager to promote the occultism within his mystical faction of the Craft, he was quite disparaging of paganism. He believed it served as a flaccid distraction from the real 'work,' and purpose of the 'People' – those of the 'Faith.'

Of the qualities that drive us to truth, perception is hailed as both instinctive and intuitive; importantly, it cannot be taught. Certain things we inherit, others we acquire. Cochrane enigmatically promoted many virtues as vital to egress. Silence above all else reigns supreme; a wise occultist utilises Silence, Will and intent to evolve. Part of the Mystery lies in understanding that Silence is not the same as Secret, and Secret is not the same as Sacred. These are all tools with which the true seeker may explore and implement the 'work.' Described in one document, the 'Witch's Compass' is compared to a highly efficient machine, requiring science to use it effectively. Simple yet quite sophisticated methods of working contrast sharply – the lack of a prescribed circle, movement in and around the working denote clear distinctions quite unknown at that time.

Truth as the Ultimate deity is witnessed and beautifully described by

Robert Cochrane in a poetic vision of blinding light in which a radiant naked goddess sits astride a horse. This and other allusions to mysticism enforce the way he desired the expression of his Craft to take form. In order to achieve this, he instigated the mentor/pupil relationship, where the Master leads the student through a maze of obfuscation. One by one the veils of illusion are lifted to reveal the Truth. Each student must see this Truth and know on every level of being its implications and resonances. Individual epiphanies result from successful connections forged through the accepting Egregore of the Clan collective. These things cannot be intellectualised, but are gained only through the work itself.

Discussing aspects of the work throughout his few articles, Cochrane presents the very nature of ritual activity as that which carries the force, as a Sudan Chair carries a Queen. It reveals the nature of the Queen through its functional form providing the arena for Her worship. Animism is referred to as the first principle of the Godhead; the mundane plane is the geography of its manifestation. The sub-conscious state is not yet developed sufficiently to discern these subtleties with full awareness; consciousness detracts, forever at play upon the plane of the lapwing.

Views on deity were remarkably philosophical, upholding a belief in the Horn (stylised crown of office rather than horned) King and a Triple form of the divine feminine known as Fate, or Ultimate Truth. Together these aspects expressed the elemental and supernal worlds, by reflex. Drawing heavily upon Greek myth and the poetic studies of Robert Graves, Cochrane attempts to describe his perception of The White or Pale-Faced Goddess, whose terrible love, devours and demands all from her devotees. Bringing life and destruction indiscriminately, her trials temper the soul into wisdom. Manifest as the Muse, her ruthless ambivalence brings desolation and desire together in a poignancy unsubtle and fierce.

Mundane trivia induced by this uncompromising mistress and the longing for release shifts the dichotomy of existence from one reality into another, forging pathways to them, even into death. All is movement and flux; there is no instant, only forever. At this point lies the cessation of existence. These mystical expressions underpin a symbiotic relationship between man and the gods. One way in which his deep reverence for the gods would manifest was in his abject insistence upon the feast being consumed away from the working area. It was the specific job of one person to ensure that several fires were kept burning around the area, one of which served as the one where feasting, sleeping and converse would take place. A profound cosmology, primarily gnostic, completed by a definitive eschatology provided a teaching of extreme beauty, originating with the initial spark of existence to where the spirit in death is carried to Her Castle to await re-incarnation.

Today the concepts of religion and spirituality have through academia become rightfully distinct, but here the word *religion* was used by him quite emphatically to affirm his profoundly spiritual beliefs, which remained mystical in nature.

> "The People are concerned with Fate. Magic and religion are aids to overcome Fate, and Fate is a cradle that rocks the infant spirit."

> *"Magic is a by product in the search for Truth and is inferior to it."*

> "Magic is the development of Will as a product of the Soul in search of Wisdom."

Magic then, is clearly presented as an afterthought! The mastery of such abilities is discovered only along the bigger journey. Most importantly, it was re-iterated time and again that such illusions were not to be obsessed over, being lapwings to the ultimate cause. He declared:

"The genuine witch is a mystic at heart."

These ideas were and are very unpopular with operatives more focussed on spell-casting and theatrical embellishment. Linked to his aversion to superstition this ruffled many feathers. He was certainly not shy in denouncing those practices he deemed as outmoded:

"To retain a primitive pattern is to corrupt mind and souls…"

During the swinging sixties, spiritualist churches and other similar organizations enjoyed some measure of revival, a phenomena that shocked and dismayed him. Fiercely anti-spiritualist, he asserted that:

"…witchcraft is NOT primarily concerned with messages or mortality gained from the dead. It is concerned with the action of God and gods upon man, and man's position spiritually…"

In other words, we should use our own will to act in accord with our daimonic guidance to seek solutions to any given problem; through direct contact with spirit rather than messages via so-called mediums. The actions of the SELF were stressed repeatedly. It was his assertion that no-one but oneself may work magic or tread the path. It remains an individual and lonely path.

"Through poetry the gods speak.
Through poetic inference they teach."

Above all other imperatives within his works, this is the premise that I find the most compelling. Woven expertly throughout his many works are disparate lines of exquisite poetry, riddles and proverbs, teeming with inherent mysticism and profound wisdom. Beyond this basic analysis, closer inspection reveals another more subtle shift permeating the beauty expounded in later works denoting a marked refinement of his earlier ideologies. This is best understood as being not so much a change of direction, as a focussed honing in on his collective works and experiences.

This refinement is more readily approached through his articles, where this trend predominates; it is less marked, but still discernible within the letters, which because they are frequently presented out of their true chronology renders this problematic. Being written to different people, the letters are constructed for distinct purposes; each set is calculated to cajole, garner and extricate information in a particular way from diverse people. Letters by their very nature express a personal directive.

Demonstrating his 'mission' with zeal, his purpose then, is passionately expressed even within the set of letters to his peer and fellow crafter, Norman Gills, whom he boldly reminds, that we are but channels for forces raised by prayer and faith, asserting that the 'power' employed is not sourced within us, but externally. Articles differ substantially from this personalised missive style, away from the singular purpose underlying the correspondence between writer and recipient for whom it is composed/designed.

By way of contrast, an article conveys *the* mission statement, *the* sermon for the masses if you will; a quite different perspective contrived within the mindset of the author. Through his few articles he released a view of the Craft as he wished it to be known, unfolding a vision that was simultaneously innovative and contentious. And so at last we may return to the crux of his belief, expounded here, unambiguous, unprecedented and un-garnished.

The Faith of the Wise, was his final submission, the last work in which he spills out his poignant yet beautiful insights. Published just five months before he found himself alone, seemingly without family, friends, work or purpose; increasing despair drove him to his death by suicide just two months later. Of all his works, this one final article crystallises his developed and refined ideology. He freely announces that in his opinion, ritual is merely a means to an end, and how he had no desire or interest in spell craft or folkloric fertility celebrations, or pagan worship of those who considered themselves to be of the 'peasantry' or rustic stock. This, he believed was a distraction from the work. In this article Cochrane promotes three carefully prioritised tenets of the **Faith**:

1 - The Faith is a vehicle for **Revelation and Union** – the gnosis of Truth

2 - The Faith is about **Devotion -** how to attain gnosis

3 - The Faith is about the actual **Nature** of mystical experience itself

Most fundamental for him with regard to the Craft, were his beliefs, described unambiguously as a religion and a serious discipline – hence '***Faith*** of the Wise.' He promoted it as a way of life, not just a practise reserved for high days and holidays! Adherents were 'of the ***Faith***.' Through its Mysteries he was adamant that man attains awareness of the 'self' as a product of God. This awareness generates change, occurring repeatedly to effect a complete re-structuring of one's life's pattern or template by which the devotee returns intermittently to the original Source, until released from its bonds.

Masterfully, he succinctly describes the distinctions between form and force as they are within his perception of 'The Faith':

Form appeals to the Mind to its intellect.

Force reveals itself in the essence of being – it is KNOWN, it is UNDERSTOOD, it is REMEMBERED.

To validate this, he asserts five separate proofs, although he is at pains to define them as not being intellectual exercises, but *experiences of force*. Stressed as empathic realisations borne of direct and unequivocal visionary contact, these are as follows:

1 **Poetic Vision** – stimulation through imagery of traditional symbols that generate intuitive *perception* in dreams and trance work (use of logic or reason considered an obstruction to this process).

2 **Vision of Memory** – process of anamnesis, of former levels of existence and the harvesting of *gnosis* achieved from them.

3 **Magical Vision** – immersion and envelopment of Kabbalistic principles; primarily, this would necessitate working with the three Mothers (Aleph, Mem and Shin) via the Three Rings of the Moat. The purpose is *Seership*, Oracular Questing and Thaumaturgy.

4 **Religious Vision** – part of a true 'Initiation'; the mystical aim of the *Vigil*. Temporary access of devotee to godhead. Wherein the Cosmology of the Mythos is realised.

5 **Mystical Vision** – in which the servant (a pilgrim, who in full humility, surrenders themselves), rather than the devotee enters full *union* with Godhead. In this, awareness of form ceases; there exists the point of force alone – *'fanaa,'* the annihilation of ego. Merkavah. Eschatology of the Mythos.

Cumulatively, these demonstrate the evolution of: **perception, gnosis, seership, vigil** (challenge/trial/surrender) **and union** (Individuation)! All five of these profound expressions are intrinsic to the Mythos, teachings and praxes of the Clan of Tubal Cain that serve to remove all doubt except upon the veracity thereafter of the so-called 'external' world. All realities become True at some level. All realities become possible to experience. Inner illumination reifies the outer form of being. Returning to the issue of secrecy, Robert Cochrane in contemplation of this vital Pentalphic formulae emphasised how the only secret regarding these five proofs, is that which makes one able to enter the ***silent*** realms of the gods. Such an enigma it is beyond expression. It is a paradox not taught by human contact. Of this he said:

> "Therefore it can be shown that the Faith is a complex philosophy dealing with the Nature of Truth, Experience and Devotion." "It requires discipline and work; plus utter and complete devotion to the common aim."

Tragically, his star rose and fell, burning fiercely leaving his work unfinished; although even this he had predicted, declaring that he was laying the groundwork for others to reap. In just a short a time, a mere two years he had found and lost everything. Here he had glimpsed the Grail, but felt unworthy to take it. In that single flash of Truth, he adhered to his own Law. In conclusion, this small paragraph unveils the essence by which all other works may be disclosed – it is the key principle to the apprehension of the Mysteries:

> "To practise genuine magic is to literally throw your life away upon imponderables and half-apparent truths that you know will never become clear until death overtakes all of us. Magic is the rejection of illusion in favour of what may be a greater illusion still."

The Stang

"... that binds the staff that is owned by the Maid..."

By right of the *'Old Covenant'* the Maid is the soul embodiment of the Clan Stang, literally! Through it a seven year cyclical leadership is imposed upon the Magister as the 'Son of the Morning Star', a title that confers a significant clue to the purpose of this particular Stang.[90] Bound by oath, the Magister as leader of the Clan is 'herald' of the Old Horn King, wielding those wisdoms intrinsic to that potency. Four such cycles are possible in a single human life span forming a cycle of Saturn somewhat appropriately as the Old Father of Time, Knowledge and Witness to Fate who wraps and binds us to and within the Will of *Hekate*. My predecessor and former Maid, the widow of Robert Cochrane is noted for bearing the 'Virtue' of the Clan, best understood at its simplest as the source link of the *Egregore*, a privilege of birth (if hereditary) or transmission if traditional.[91] This invites us to ponder more deeply upon the nature of the Stang and the Maid, their relationship to it and each other, supplemented by literary sources, both historical and mythological.

We may begin that search quite specifically with the underrated and little understood concept of the Staff /Stang as the sacred and literal *'Tree of Life,'* both of knowledge *and* immortality, encompassing all variants of the *Axis Mundi*, the metaphoric pole, ladder, or tree, pivotal to the starry heavens and the fiery abyss. The species of tree is unimportant as it shifts according to location and culture. Invariably these choices will determine the renown of that tree for its longevity, fecundity and powers of prophesy. Hence it could be the Yew in Saxony, the Ash in Norway and the much revered Oak in Italy and across Europe. In Chaldea, the Date-palm was unequalled for its sacred regard, so too the Fig-tree in India and a vine in Assyria. Other fruits of sacred trees include apples, peaches, pomegranates and even cherries. Before we embark upon this journey it is noteworthy that the oldest book of Western religion asserts how the serpent typically offers Adam *through Eve*, the 'fruit' of the Tree of Wisdom and Immortality. Cogently, in that archaic world, such a sacred tree as the simulacra of Nature was imbued with the actual presence of the Goddess, the '*asherîm,*' exuding wisdom through that Virtue.[92] So how did the world forget Her so easily; how did Her primacy become so redundant, preserved among the Craft and some occult lodges whose heterodox perspective retained Her mystery?

Humanity's obsession with eschatological matters of life, death and the nebulous 'other' causes us to strive for gnosis, the wisdom to prevail the course and trial of our lives, that we may ultimately transcend them as concerns, becoming secure in the certainty of a known 'otherness.' With this view, it is clearly impossible to accept the separation of a *'Tree of Knowledge'* from a *'Tree of Life.'* One is both a function and foundation of the other, intrinsic to its mutual purpose. Of course, there is nothing so certain as a closed mind, especially in the acceptance or expectance of clear delineations so essential for our perceived 'security.'

But, just as the land does not end upon the horizon, the Tree does not sit upon it; the roots breach through the chthonic realms and its branches the various elevations of the *sub-luna* realms. Water seeps into the so-called liminal shoreline boundaries. Separation is both artificial and illusory, a design motif of mundane convenience. Fruit is borne upon this Tree, nourished by the waters laving at its root. Consumed by mankind it imparts life, death and knowledge; wisdom occurs when these mysteries are absorbed in good measure, explored appropriately and given

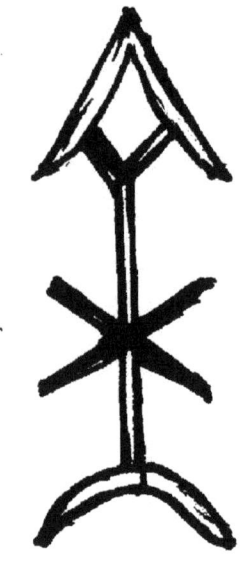 

SUMERIAN CYLINDER SEALS – ARCHAIC STAFFS

practical application. They are not yielded lightly and the quest for enlightenment is perilous at best and inimical at worst.

Once committed, we become drawn into a dizzying cosmic game as we traverse the *'Holy Tree of Gnosis'* dependent upon our observations and interactions, being very much subject to how we hold and shake the dice we are given.[93] Do we act from desire or will? Is it perhaps need or simply opportunity? Temptation hangs from the Tree yielding both the honey-sweet dew of life, but also the sour poison of death. Eve does not hesitate; she reaches up to grasp her certain prize, her own gift to herself. Willingly the challenge is accepted, expressed by the serpent, the psychopomp within this enigmatic triad. For this, woman is presented as the beguiler, the tempter, ironically representing illusion itself. Yet this illusory form opens Adam's eyes; equally as Mara, she enabled Buddha to perceive the keys to his enlightenment.

Phoenician cosmological tradition records the belief across the Mediterranean basin into the Near East, how the first race of beings worshipped plants venerating them as gods and demi-gods, often depicting them initially as stylised form that later developed into simpler and more graphic representations more indicative of their sacrificial purpose. Symbolic horns, crowns and even wings were attributes fashioned into their visual and written narratives. Upon these holy trees, the stars themselves, the winds and the heavens hung as adornments, even as their roots motioned the seas and waters of the Earth.[94] Such hoary examples of the template that formed the latter-day Yggdrasil are quite revelatory in that they personify the *female rather than the male* element commonly acceptable to recent and possibly erroneous interpretation in my estimation. Another curious image survives upon one cylinder seal that enigmatically suggests a possible pre-cursor of the Maypole. Plaited whipcords dangle from horn-like branches that crown a tall pole.[95] Similar carvings illustrate winged hoops suspended above the pole, which as absolute symbols infer again the enigmatic I and O of divinity, given as letters, sonics and sexual graphics.

Numerous myths highlight divine ladies who became 'transformed' into trees. Iconic stele carved in wood and stone litter museums across the world as testament to the absolute function of the divine female in tree stumps and rounded or conical stones. Though frequently mistaken as phallic, they were rarely considered as such. Most significant still, are the trees upon and within which heroes and demi-gods are interred; Attis is but one example. Best perhaps of all is the myth of Osiris, awaiting his resurrection within the wooden chest of 'Isis.' Another more recent myth relates how *Nimuë* (cogently) imprisons Merlin within the trunk of a tree, the manifest shell of her magical 'other.'

Of immense significance to this exploration is a 16th century woodcut depicting the '*Fall and Redemption of Man*' by Cranach the Younger. It portrays the *Axis Mundi* or central omphalos as an oak tree, the staggering relevance of which will soon become apparent as our Odyssey progresses. Fragile, withered branches straggle the left side of this tree, and to the right, fresh green shoots sprout, rejuvenated by the blood of Christ, spurting from his wound. To the left of this image Adam and Eve stand shamed in Eden, land of the '*Old Covenant*,' partaking of the forbidden fruit; to the right, they are shown invigorated through the '*New Covenant*' of Christ's sacrifice.[96]

Context reveals everything it is said, and the primal gods of the archaic world are herein presented, preserving the cosmology of the 'Clan of Tubal Cain' and its eschatology inviting true seekers to walk again in Eden. How we achieve that sublime destiny is a task that focuses upon the Stang as a pivotal key. The Staff or Stang as a Holy Tree is attested as the point of sacrifice in deed and principle by numerous religious analogies and mythological allegories, sharing the fundamental tenet of willing surrender by the male hero/priest/king to the *'Tree' of life/death/wisdom*. Essentially, the Stang is the perfumed altar, the active point of sacrifice as the iconic embodiment of the Clan's triune deity. Implying so much more, the following masks are given by both Robert Cochrane and E.J. Jones as 'close approximations' to this triune figure of: Saturn, (Old Horn King); Hekate (Wisdom and Virtue) and Hermes (Young Horn King) forming the father, mother, child triad common to many religious beliefs.[97]

A startling precedent exists that utilises the symbol of the Stang to articulate aspects of the divine Feminine as the '*Asherah Pole,*' the axial hub and catalyst for tribal cosmology. Asherah literally means 'bride of God' and is traceable to at least 2000 BCE confirming Her role as the chief power of *El*. She is '*Asherah of the Sea,*' the formative *Stella Maris*, stating Her domain as the watery Earth, and whose milk nourished the *Ba'als, Lugals* and *Yahu*s across the Near and Middle East.[98] Taking the iconic form of a single carved stave, the *Asherah* pole is directly cognate with the sacred tree of *Inanna*, which through its ideogram adopted the symbolic forms of a reed bundle and the stone pillar that replaced it. But the stylised form of the carving is only inferred, leaving us to surmise all other relevant possibilities. This carved stave received blessings, incense and other offerings daily. Once again, historical annals of spiritual and religious evolution are tantalisingly peppered with clues that hint to the required context: as ever, it is always hidden in plain sight!

Solomon was much criticised for raising altars to her and to *Ba'al*, yet they were both maintained even into the 7th century BCE. Aaron's rod indicated lawful investiture and similarly, Moses secured his own authority through a 'brazen serpent' named '*Nehushtan*.' Theologians have long speculated on the meritable probability of the twin tablets of Moses

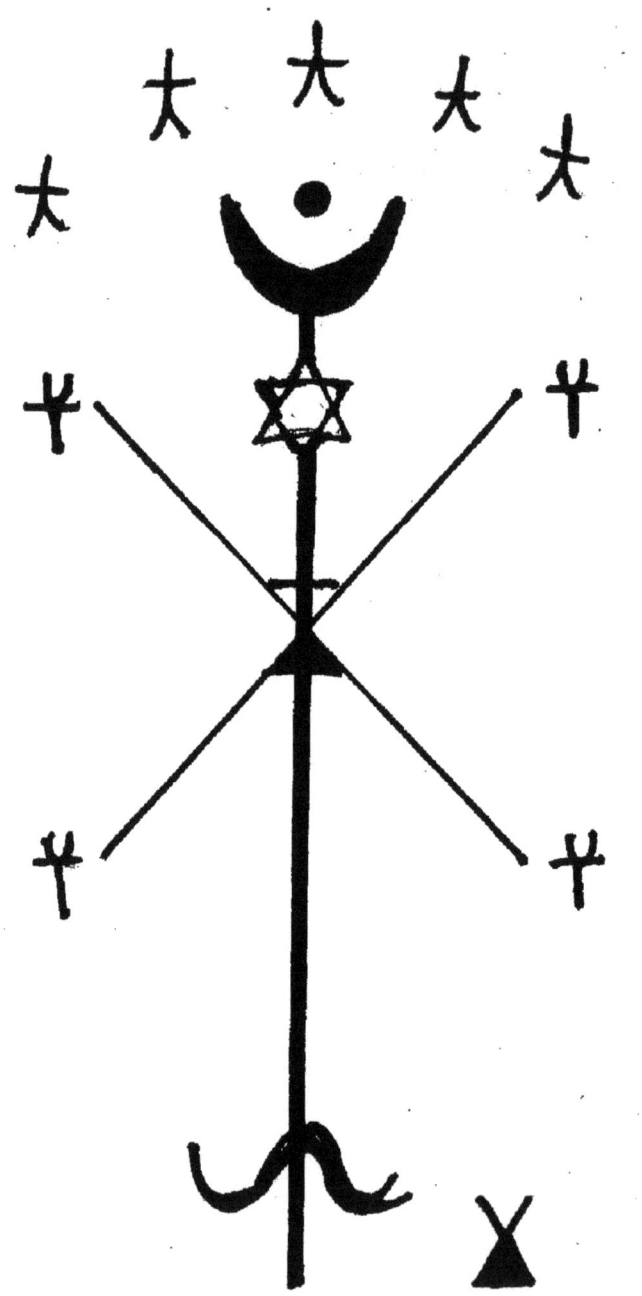

Roy's Star Stang – Clan Cosmology

being stone ensigns of the Masculine and Feminine aspects of deity, reminiscent of the divine *Mé,* the Sacred and Mundane Laws and their attendant Virtues of ancient Sumer. It is not unreasonable to extrapolate further the possibility of these two stone tablets taking form as the legendary Twin Pillars of Tubal Cain, each a repository of knowledge, lore and law. Such effects would generate the cumulative Virtue of a gate betwixt them into the '*Holy of Holies*,' entered only the High Priest, whose emblem would naturally be the Staff (hand) or full Stave (Stang).

Similarly, all holy and sacred thresholds typically became aspected by two such pillars, stylised as arching curves, like the horns of a cow. Moreover, the cattle byre as Inanna's domain was protected by a gate of bound reeds hinged and locked between two further reed bundles. This also supports the suggestion of Her embodiment as the sublime gateway/ entrance and enclosure/sanctuary. Notable scholars have opined that both the curling reed clusters and the arched posts may imply the horns of the ram and cow respectively, having associations with particular Middle Eastern and Mediterranean deities. Linked particularly to the shifting Virtue of divine light in its lunar, solar and celestial forms, they are perceived in the representations of night and day as the polarised forces of life and death.[99] Images survive depicting her adorned face either atop a curved horned pillar or more commonly as the physical embodiment of the tree itself.

Other glyphs have developed the identity of the 'Tree of Life': primarily, these are the triangle and the tau cross. Another, yet more significant, is the ankh, referred to as the 'Key of Life.' The Indus valley has awarded us a beautiful seal that portrays, very simply the bull deity in front of a horned female deity within a tree whose branches also curve sympathetically up and outwards as horns. Cedars and other sacred trees were the oracles of Heaven and Earth; moreover a certain kind of divination known as *phyllomancy* (so favoured by both E.J.J. & R.C.) where the divine breath spoke as the winds rustling through the leaves, imparting its secrets and wisdoms.[100]

She is the zoomorphic Mistress of the wild beasts and protectress of Her kine, flocks and herds, standing guard between them, separating order from chaos; another important aspect of her role. These gateways become referred to as the *'Gate of Horn'* and were deemed as the entrance to chthonic realms of the dead and of all spirits. Later designs for temple complexes whether simple mounds or the more sophisticated *Temenos*, drew inspiration from this principle that continued to honour the divine feminine as gateway and threshold of other worldly realms. Here we begin to form a clear link to the horned deities and the Underworld of later eras. Twin peaks exampled in *Saffron, Meru, Kailash, Moriah* and *Kildare* became sacred visual expressions of Her presence on this manifest plane, a cherished reflection of the Celestial divine, Her twin and unseen 'other.' Known as the two Gates of the Mysteries, the Twin Pillars assume the terrestrial Southern Gate of Man for Initiatory ascent at the Summer Solstice and the Celestial Northern Gate of Divinity for the birth and descent of the Avatar.[101]

Depicted as the nurturing, sacred and Holy Cow whose 'milk' nourishes king, pauper or beast, *Hat-Hor* is the finest known exemplar among a dazzling array of early star deities, that includes *Astarte, Tanit, Elath, Ishtar, Nuit* and *Neith* the *'Mother of the Sun'* and also *Asherah*, Mother of the Divine twins of the Morning and Evening stars - *Shahar*/Venus and *Shalem*/Mercury. All were honoured in sacred enclosures upon and within the mountains and mounds of Her entitled domain. As the 'cleft' in the mountain, Her *'Gate of Horn'* divides *"the death sleep from the waking Sun."* Caves, especially those facing westwardly (the perceived direction of death) were deemed particularly sacred, as the belly from which She restored life to the dead. She is in fact the vehicle and means by which the male avatar descends to Earth. Hat-Hor was once considered manifest in the milky turquoise desert stones, highly prized for their affinity with this archaic Goddess form. A Sumerian text says of (the Lady of the Mountain): *'She who gives life to the dead'* specifically where such a male deific principle is generally given as her 'son':

> "...the first among the divinities who mourn the dying god is Geshar (Nin) Khursagga thy mother..."

These gifts then are her fruits, the produce of her own body as the *'Tree of Life and Death,'* finding a common depiction as the *'Goddess of the Sycamore'* (a type of date palm) in ancient Egypt. The Sycamore likewise yields its milk to feed the dead by whom the living becomes its fruit. On another cylinder seal, Tammuz (as the Sun/son) is shown being released from his mountain tomb, the actual body of the Divine Creatrix Herself in the form of a tree known as *'Kishkanu'* or *'Tree of the Underworld.'* What is even more interesting, the shadow formed by this tree nurtures both *Shamash* and *Tammuz* as two rival yet complementary Winter and Summer solar deities.[102] Again we may note that numerous myths require the incarceration of the king/hero/priest's body to be literally enfolded within the barque or 'trunk' of a tree, before re-generation by Her **'*leafy*** breath.'

Many kings and heroes of this period were said to be the lovers or 'shepherds' of *Inanna*: She who dwells within the *'House of Light'* as the divine Shekinah, the first and primal manifestation in *Malkuth* as daughter and threshold to Kether. This is immensely significant to the axial points upon the pole/tree. All lovers of *Inanna* received some small measure of wisdom for their attentions. Yet it is recorded that Her own great love and twin was the 'farmer.' Like the sublime *Sophia, Inanna/Ishtar* is the mother of seven gods (*sebittu*). Reductionism brings all back to the simple cognate forms of farmer (evolution) and shepherd (stasis), reflecting

Lady of the Sycamore

countless archaic myths of rival 'twins' who retain this dynamic. *Cain* the farmer is qualified by the sickle and Abel as the pastoral shepherd, by a ram.

Abel was later replaced by the serpent in the Ophite Gnostic cult that also highly revered Sophia, the hypostatized form of *Chockmah - Sophia Prounicos*, the *serpent of the tree*. She embodies the mysteries, salvation and redemption in the Supernal Triad where she is the voice of the Father ('I am the light of thought'), the speech of the Mother ('I am the expression of thought') and the word of the *Christos* ('I am the unification and assimilation of both voice and speech,' given as the revelation of the One Truth -Vac). She descends three times as a male, as a female and as the Holy Spirit. In this final form, She relates to our *'Lady who will gather us up Home again,'* back to the spinning Castle of *Caer Sidi* - the eternal kingdom. *Caer Sidi* turning upon a hill is swifter than all the Winds. It is the seat of resplendent fire, the divine throne in this realm of spirit. Many legends claim this seat perilous as the Devil's chair, Arthur's chair, Druid's chair etc. – the holy omphalos, and dancing stone of the Goddess.[103]

Baptism, or immersion into Her stream of words/wisdom generates the necessary anamnesis to cross the Lethe to reach Her High abode. An Ophitic tenet asserts a triad of Man (god), Son of Man, (heavenly Adam) and third man (Seth): Seth (masc & fem case) is ambiguously male, the other two are deemed androgynous. One other Gnostic text discusses *Norea* and *Seth*, brother and sister as twins analogous to *Tubal* and *Namaah*. Curiously, *Namaah* appears in both Sanskrit and Hebraic, both meaning beautiful or beloved one. She is the feminine counterpart, the manifest wisdom of Tubal, who is erroneously presented, I believe, as a triplicity with *Jubal* and *Jabal*. Sharing the same root, they are descriptives for his three distinct qualities, of smith craft, music and the agriculture. So the puzzle begins to form a pattern of repeated events and structure.

Divinities imparted their Virtue to mortals through various regal tools, the finest being the Crown, formed of tiered layers of curved horns, emblematic of the totemic and primal animals to whom homage was given. Countless cylinder seals from ancient Sumer portray images of divine females, crowned with horns, guarding beasts both wild and domestic, but also grain. The Crown She bestowed upon the early priest-kings when 'Kingship was lowered from Heaven' is both gate and key to the realms the gods inhabit. Such examples were repeated for millennia depicting the divine feminine again as the force of life and death, and the divine masculine as the form it manifests upon and within the Earth (Her 'body'). Setting contextual sacrificial and fertility myths aside for the moment, we must focus instead upon the concept of her being the force behind his form and the Virtue She holds to impart life and death within Her geographically specific sanctuaries, emulated by man as mounds, pyramids and ziggurats sharing the time-honoured design of *twin posts* for the threshold. Free standing posts, unhampered by structure lend credence to the purpose of this beyond that of practical engineering.

Sacred enclosures including hypnogogic incubation cells increased the use of natural caves as designated spaces for the actuation and celebration of the '*Hieros Gamos*.' Here the celebrants assembled to ritualise acts of sowing and reaping of the life generating seed, enriched and fecundated by that process. From this Neolithic drama the solar and lunar potencies became united and fêted, symbolised by the Staff, the arc/crescent and the star or lunate cross. These form the simple graphic used by the '*Clan of Tubal Cain*' many hundreds of years later to represent the Stang.

Another form of evolutionary renewal draws inspired wisdoms

through the body of the Creatrix in Her guise as the 'Tree of Knowledge'; *Odhin* is the finest example of this. In Sumerian Temples, the *'Great Binding Post'* connected Heaven and Earth, initiating the development of spiral circuits typical of later Ziggurats, each realm of ascent and descent marked for the celestial telesmia appropriate to it. In remembrance of the 'Crown' bestowed upon the early priest–kings of Sumer, it was the sacred duty of each king to build not only a temple as a dwelling place for their tutelary deity (each city nominated one for themselves), but to ensure continued and dedicated focus upon principle points of access, noted and honoured by all. In accord with this, Assyrian tablets confirm their understanding of their forebears in awarding the *'Lady of Eden'* the revealing epithet: *'Goddess of the Tree of Life.'*[104]

Another intriguing facet to this complex puzzle lies in the Chaldean word for (tree) 'wood of life' - *ges-tin,* which prefixes *Inanna* in Her descent myth, where as *Gestinanna* she is named as the 'sister' of *Dumuzzi*. Her descent is perceived as a needful search for the fructifying and rejuvenating *'Waters of Life,'* the natural springs and rivers of the plains of Sumer, not watered by the alluvial clouds of Europe. For Her, the great pool, the Absu lies below. She, like the others is a willing sacrifice to Herself until a replacement can be found to continue this aspect of Her manifest earthly powers concerned with the dead and the re-animating of the dead.

> "O thou who art adorable, who givest salvation, life and justice, vivify my name."[105]

Of considerable import is the Mythopoetic view of the Sun's apparent rising each day from the clefted mountain – *'The Gate of Horn,'* the body of his Mother, the Earth. The Sun also conducted an annual and seasonal ascent/descent out of and into Her 'body' via the Tree of the Underworld, the Shadow of *Shamash* and *Tammuz*. As the 'shepherd' gave way to the 'farmer,' the *'Holy Barque'* played host to 'Virtue,' of a god returning to its Source of re-generation. Emulating this potent instrument of all elements of and within the Earth He became subverted by 'The Ploughman,' reflected in the Heavens by the man-faced lion (emblem of the Sun) with his plough. In this way, the movement of the Sun is mirrored in the seasons of the Earth, assuming greater significance under the invading Semitic Akkadians.

All columnar forms, be they tree, monolith, gate or barque have undeniably represented Her as the Divine potency, the one constant in a landscape of flux. Standing stones exampled by the sacred stele of Byblos may mark the annular solar movement, fixing to the Earth erect signatures denoting the celebrated union of Heaven and Earth. However, as we have determined, not all stone tumuli are to be understood as phallic or male, many of them depict the wooden stave, or reed pillar associated with *Inanna* as the *'Bab ilu'* or divine gate. Whether erect or recumbent, these enigmatic stone markers became noted and used as literal hearths, the manifest presence of divine grace – the altar and foci of worship.[106] They frequently served a secondary function as Steles of Law, expressing divine decrees, as witnessed and upheld by their Leaders in the form of Priests, Priest-Kings and Kings.

Eventually this generated the concept of the *'Covenant,'* a particular agreement binding a King to his kin and vice versa, but more importantly, through him to their tutelary deity. Known as the *'Old Covenant'* through Jacob as the 'Stone of Israel,' it is distinguished from the *'New Covenant'* wherein Peter the 'rock' had aspired to that role of mediatrix. The *'Beth-el'* or stone of God finds its origins in this concept, later subject to complex anointing rituals by blood and oil for all kinsmen, sharing this binding by oath as a belonging through the blood. The etymology of Yoseph was later scrutinised by biblical scholars, who proposed that a phonetic rendering of his name expresses the prefix *IO*, meaning Divine Mother (Greek) alongside *Cephas* (also Greek) for stone, giving: Mother Stone. So perhaps the passages may arguably refer to particular precedents that relate to Jesus as 'son' of '*Yoseph*,' significantly a priest bound to the Virtue of the Holy Mother? Possibly?

Jacob apparently marked the sacred spot where his stone pillow rested with an *oak tree* to denote his visionary ascent to the heavens via the ladder. Beneath this symbolic 'ladder' he buried holy relics, further empowering the spot as one of communion between the beings of the Heavens and the Earth. Later, along his pilgrimage Jacob erected a more permanent pillar of stone and a cairn as a more fitting habitat for the divine, to be invoked by prayer, sacrifice and offerings. Oaths were taken before it, bound in the sacrament of the precursor for the Eucharist.[107] Out of this developed a less exclusive notion of a binding[108] as one in the 'spirit' of a people, better expressed as the (ancestral) Egregore of the nation. Totemic stones came to indicate the identity of distinct tribes or clans with an overarching people, best exemplified most pertinently in the '*Choshen*' (Breastplate) worn by the Israelite Priests where Kenotheistic unity was eventually formulated, favouring one Supreme tribal god above all others. It became an imperative for any anointed King to receive his coronation over the ancestral stone, the representative of law, as given and held through and by the manifest divine presence within it. Thusly did possession of it come to signify the rightness and justness of any monarch to rule; Her Virtue passing to him. The omphalos of Delphi, stone of scone, Arthur's round table and the *Ka'aba* are all cultural exemplars of this extraordinary concept.

In the Neolithic world She had been a stone block, a throne a mount to represent the bond between Man and Creatrix. Her presence was quite graphically one that enthroned and enveloped the Monarch within

Her status. As She was Night, Death and the Sacrificial altar, the King on assuming Her Horned crown became, Light, Life and Redemption. Temporal power shifted and the prevailing animism was deemed simplistic and superstitious by Prophets who railed incessantly against it. Perceived as corruptions of the Sacred Pillars depicting the Tree of Life and Death and the Tree of Knowledge, Temples and their Icons were torn down:

> "sacrifice shifted from blood to burnt offerings, from propitiation to bribe, communion to bequest, from reciprocity to bargain..."[109]

Symbols from the archaic world hold many keys to our understanding the deeper layers of these images. From the rich language of the Phoenicians, many letters have acquired iconic status. Most relevant to the 'Tree' theme explored here, is the *Tau*, meaning the fiery light or spirit and presence of God in fact. As '*Zethau*' it takes the form of a double Tau, the glyph for sword and tree.[110] It is clearly unsurprising how the T shaped Tau became the original emblem for the resurrection of both Osiris and Jesus.

Horned Lions, more than being solar beasts or heraldic emblems are significant guardians of Her tree, often conversely, chthonic, and transmute into winged Genii as priestly mediators to Her devotees. Assyrian bas-reliefs depict ceremonial propagation by these zoomorphic wind spirits of a central Holy 'Tree,' in whose hands, phallic cones tend and fertilise the stylised form and earthly body of the *Axis Mundi*, the Creatrix Herself. Enclosures and shrines reveal the force of the divine Creatrix, presiding over the mortal remains in the form of the horned pillared gateway. Shrines composed of stones or trees were the sacrosanct areas of Her consumption and re-generation of souls across Minos, Crete, Greece, Asia, Egypt and Sumer.

These later became stylised totemic beasts, hence Her association with all horned animals, not necessarily of the Hunt, but as guardians representing Herself. Numerous 19th and early 20th century anthropologists and mythographers continued the associative trend where women were equated with the virtue of *'naturae'* and men with the virtue of culture and its incumbent civilising arts.[111] Time is after all 'Father' to the *'Queen of Truth.'*[112] As Sophianic mistress She is twined with Her other vital role as the *'Axis Mundi.'*[113] Maze dances held on the threshing floors of archaic plains celebrate fecundity on all levels the patterns of life and death, of the sacred marriage through the spiral weaving to and from the centre unceasingly, this description is reminiscent of the poetic definitions of *Caer Sidi* by Robert Cochrane of:

> 'the Castle that spins without motion'
> and of: 'the Cauldron that is never still.'[114]

Within earlier Palaeolithic societies, recumbent stones deemed to be Her body, personified in the earthen altar in the fullest sense. These continue to serve as the central focus of many dwellings as hearthstones. Charged within the *'Old Covenant,'* the Maid as 'bride' of the Old Horn King is represented by the Hearthstone, binding her spirit with His to the Stang she holds, transmuting its Virtue to her Clan, a cohesive unit for its survival and continuity. In this manner, the *'House that Jack Built'* becomes through the son/Sun, embodied within the figure of the Maid as refuge for the Egregoric spirit.[115]

The woven 'knot' is therefore perfectly suited in purpose as the emblem of Inanna atop her reed pillar forming a somewhat idiosyncratic *'ankh'* also a symbol for the Virtue of life. Co-incidentally, this binding of the elements within a sacred enclosure is denoted by the graphic for salt, Earth and the gateway known as *Malkuth* in the *Kabbalah*. Magically, it represents the circle of arte and by reflux; some occultists perceive it as *'Daath'* the Gateway to the Supernal realms. Hekate is the three-fold gateway to Heaven, Earth and the Underworld, leading into the fourth realm of enlightenment; beyond Time,[116] placed in the Halls of the Gods, the poetic Castle residing spiritually in *Ceugent*.[117]

An interesting parallel to this is mimicked in the Temple or Cave (birthplace to many mystic kings, heroes, and demi-gods) referred to as the House of the Mountain wherein Heaven and Earth become bonded. This again reflects the roles of both *Inanna* and *Hat-Hor* as '*Lady of the Mountain*' spanning both the Earth and the Heavens. They are in fact examples of the Holy or Celestial Cow, Her horns support the moon above; Her legs and feet the Earth below. All that lies in between is life and death who find ingress and egress from the cleft between Her legs, the pillars that form the eternal gateway to the all things including the death-sleep of the Sun. Hence, poetically She is both 'womb and tomb.'[118] She is thus, Night and death; He is Light, life and the guide to all freedoms– *Moksha*. As 'star mother of the shepherd' *Ashtaroth* meaningfully governs Her flocks through His ministry.

Poets and artists have long grappled with concepts that motivate us at these primary and primal levels of concern, often grafting one idiom onto another with astonishing brilliance or utter and abject whimsy, almost always delineating clear boundaries between tree, serpent and Eve. Preserved in Kabbalism, these survive as the *Otz Chim*, the '*Tree of Life*' whose left and right branches encapsulated the feminine and masculine virtues of Severity and Mercy (*Joachim* and *Boaz*). These two pillars, reach upwards through the three manifest worlds, into the fourth plane of divine archetypes and non-being. It is effectively the paradisial *Huluppa* tree of Inanna, spanning the Underworld, the Earth and the Heavens, inhabited by creatures of the winds, the Earth, waters and seas all taking succour. It is essentially a '*World Tree*' that encompasses a cultural and religious cosmology relating the story of creation through the civilization of its people under the ascendance of Kingship. Again we find cognates in the Saxon *Irminsul* and the Norse *Yggdrasil*.

Another profound example is present within the three distinct pillars of *'Otz Chim,'* the Hebraic World Tree, believed to represent the *'Old Covenant'* through Adam and Eve as the twin outer pillars between which a third, of the Messiah/Saviour and Redeemer yet to come is accepted already by Christians through the *'New Covenant.'* For considerable disparate Craft Traditions, this central pillar represents the Stang, the Staff or body of the Mother upon which each of us must 'hang' – the only true and valid sacrifice. Shifting this thought onwards would therefore imply that we are our own redeemer, our own sacrifice and our own saviour. As d' Alviella astutely opines:

> "This tree has been thought to be the simulacrum of the solar god; it seems to me more logical to seek therein the symbol of the matrix in which Atys (sic) awaits his annual resurrection."[119]

This confirms that first we must find our way to Her through Him. Yet is this concept a natural or even a rational one? Certainly their mutual inter-dependence pronounces a less than subtle clue regarding the fluidity of these enforced distinctions. Remembering that the ambivalence of absolute sentience is the unifying core around which all mysteries revolve and evolve, entwining illusory duality within the *Tao*, we can investigate a divine harmonic further through states of perception less persuaded by media bias. Hypnogogic states blur certain distinctions apparent in mundane realities, where, presented as dualities all states become polarised into opposition. Paradoxically, hypnogogia serves equally well to clarify such obfuscations noted best in waking consciousness. Wrought with metaphoric symbolism, this dichotomy crystallises the nucleus of the mysteries.

The sacred and Holy Eye of Heaven flows through the *'Three Rings'* composed of the *Adityas (the holy ones)* operating in the celestial or upper level of the three active realms of the Tree; the Vayu which translate as Winds, operate on the intermediary level as the aspirative breath and psychic will. The Hearth of Agni is by this act manifest within the terrestrial realms of man, where its Virtue binds all to this 'Singular' qutub vortex. The central Sun Door or Stone of Illumination is the Heart of the Beloved, the point of Truth that permeates the three levels of being and the Three Rings as the emotive experiences that are intuitive, inexpressible, incommunicable. Osmosis leaches the Un-manifest seed into the Manifest, radiating out through the kalas of perfection. These three '*yods*' are the fiery shin, the potentiality of the Shekinah; thus we have the Eye of the Heart, the central seed point; the Eye of Stone, the manifest Graal below and the 3rd Eye of the Divine Mind above. Shamen and other workers who make their shift through trance operatives become adept manipulators of the Graal stone, the hypothalamus – the Holy of Holies fed by the free flowing nadis rising upwards into the flanking pituitary and pineal glands.

These form three coterminous dimensional sections of the Stang as described (and allegedly drawn) by Robert Cochrane and E.J. Jones, the unformed Singularity that crowns the synthesis of the equilibrating duality. Certain glyphs taken from archaic sources share considerable similarities to these drawings and bear close scrutiny. The triskele trident is the true symbol of virtue, possessing three spear points, indicative of the three levels of being, one for each level attained, one each for the mothers, one each for the set of winds and one for each of the three pillars of the trinity. With regard to its secular status, the virtues of Commerce and Industry assigned to the archaic staff of Hermes that once combined the flail and the crook as emblems of farming and pastoral dynamics mankind once depended upon are yet retained because:

"..even in the matter of symbols nothing dies which deserves to live, and is capable of transformation."[120]

And so through Her the 'Tree' becomes a fundamental, yet universal and eternal symbol of the Mysteries. No other glyph has been used so graphically, so poetically or assigned so many metaphors to convey the inherent Truth, whispered across the rustling leaves, Her breath, hissing as the serpent, ready to strike at the core of ego. From *Otz Chim* to the Holy Rood; from the Burning Bush to the *Bodhi* Tree or even from the *Gardh* trees[121] to the *Qliphoth*, the spirit of Truth, Love and Beauty may be experienced through the vitality of the *Axis Mundi*, effectively the *Anima Mundi* too.

Another Indus Valley seal circa 2000BCE presents a seductive cameo of a Horned Goddess amidst a sacred fig-tree (*pipal*); seven attendants line-up as an eighth, possibly male, wearing a very elaborate horned head-dress, bows before the Tree. Small carvings of what appear to be birds, fish and kine surround the Tree behind and above Her.[122] This recurring image features across the Near and Far East, Egypt and the Mediterranean. Scriptural allegory weaves the tale of the 'Fig Tree' that bore no fruit, having only the outward sign of fecundity in its golden leaves, revealing the purpose of the Tree as yet unrealized. The word for this principle of apprehension with regard to the unfilled lack yet to be manifest is '*Gardh*'.[123] So a *Gardh* tree is one that retains the pleromic essence, the presence and promise of this realization. We then, are the fruit of the Tree, needing the guidance and infusion of wisdom from the divine breath at play in the leafy boughs of Eden and all its earthly counterparts, or *Gardh*-trees.

Curiously, *Alah*, the word noted for God throughout the Islamic world originates in the stem meaning a leafy bough. In the sense of this particular golden bough, carrying all the virtue and potential of 'God,' it becomes extremely profound! The Islamic mystic, Ibn 'Arabi wrote of the *'Tree of Being'* that if we were to view the whole of creation as a tree, then its virtue resides in its seed - the fruit, which cultivated becomes a self-perpetuating forest over time, all contained within the one primal seed from which all life sprang. Thus he said: *"the fruit of a tree is the result of its seed."*[124] He goes on to describe the tree as reaching into all realms; we reside within the bark sheltered by the divine leafy boughs of the arc of the heavens where the *secret of the word is hidden*; its nourishing sap inspires all creatures partaking of that virtue. Surrounding this *'Tree of Being'* are the stars of the heavens, night and day are worn as covers, black and white, giving light and the hidden light that hides the throne around which the angels dwell mediating twixt ourselves and the divine Source.[125]

Within the Mabinogion, the principle of duality is depicted in the 'split tree,' a startling visual dynamic of unparalleled simplicity that conveys the dualism of life and death. Though wisdom here is less clearly represented; it has to be worked for. Ever illusive, the arboreal anima requires subtle engagement to fully syncretise its gems. This is precisely what Buddha did, in fact. Emaciated and near death, Gautama laid beneath its leafy boughs contemplating his Fate, when he became subject to weird and wonderful visions. Many interpretations have been offered of this benign parable, and yet I add one more to the increasing cache, for others beyond me to explore.

Drawing upon personal insight and experience, I may confirm the inexorable mystical link between death and love. Death comes as a lover, painfully sensitive and beautiful to seduce away your soul. Entranced we are led by this spectral shadow across the threshold, enjoined to follow hither into the walled garden of *Paradisio*. Eastern traditions assign this duty to a beautiful maiden. In the West, She transmutes into whatever we most fear and least expect - a generic spirit lover, the grim reaper, a scheming seductress, a siren or harpy whose mission it is to steal our souls.

According to the Upanishads, the divine essence must remain unknowable within an eternity. Truth also is beyond mortal kenning and is similarly classified as unknowable. All who seek the mystery of the eternal Truth must invest in the *Pistis Sophia* – or the Faith of Wisdom, (the reality of the conscious mind) the release given, where attained, denies the material reality of construct so liberates itself from the principle of illusion (the reality of the sub-conscious mind), hence Robert Cochrane placed '*Truth*' beyond the Gods.

But what is Truth and how then is it recognised? The '*Akincanayatana*' or '*Void*' is the realm of nothingness – it is neither being nor non-being but a state of Truth that transcends the cycle of life, death and rebirth; the Wisdom to be free of this wheel is now obtained. Within the seduction of the illusion that faces us all in that final moment is concealed the kernel of truth, visible to those whose eyes have acquired the requisite sensitivity to detect this much sought prize.

Very few pass this ordeal, indeed the Buddha records that he almost succumbed to the breath-taking beauty of a vision that sought to obfuscate the right of destiny from him. Robert Cochrane was perhaps one of the few people to appreciate this principle and understand its mystery sufficiently to attempt to convey it through his teachings. In fact Cochrane asserted the Stang as being:

'The single path towards enlightenment.'[126]

He considered it to be no less than a whole cosmology, reflected upon its simple glyph:

"**Stang:** The Horse. It is the supreme implement. It represents the Middle Pillar of Yggdrasil. The Ash at one end, the Rowan at the other. Its roots are

Malkuth, or the Gateway, that is physical experience. It should be forked and bound at the base with iron. The Gateway because it is phallic and represents Hermes the Guide, and divides into these aspects as it rises.

The **Moon** because it is the path to the Mysteries. The Foundation of Wisdom and spiritual experience.
[Saturn]

It is **Love** because it represents the union of male and female, therefore attraction and counter-attraction, and it is beauty, the child of Wisdom (Horn Child).
[Hermes]

It is **Death**. The transformation. The next attribute at the Horns is the Goddess or primal movement up to the position of death, then it becomes the single path of enlightenment."
[Hekate]
(Robert Cochrane)[127]

The Stang holds the spirit of the Young Horn King, the fusion of Love, Beauty and Wisdom or Truth – a Triune altar. Facing North, in the Mound section of the Clan compass, the Stang is here articulated as the 'Tree':

Element of Air, the Stang is sevenfold:

- ❖ Hermes the Guide: Caduceus
- ❖ Moon pathway of the Mysteries: the Nightmare of nocturnal oneiric experience

❖ Foundation of wisdom and spiritual experience (mystical experience within the tangs): Equilibrium of *bhakti* and *gnana*

❖ Love because it is the union of male and female: *Merkavah*

❖ Beauty as the Child of Wisdom: Horn Child

❖ Death as the final Transformation: the *Buraq*, or vehicle of Grace

❖ Primal movement: the qutub point denoting enlightenment

As Death it is the Tau or altar of sacrifice. Most commonly, this tree is given as Oak, the sacred tree of many Northern traditions, but also in others in warmer climes as the *'Holm'* Oak. Indeed the Magister's 'hand-staff' held by grace of the Maid, bears a totem animal 'hung' upon it denoting this particular sacrificial aspect to her and the Virtue vested in her as representative of the divine *Leukothea*. Every seven years, he is required to render to Her a blood price offered up to the Clan Stang that bears Her emblem, the crossed arrows of *Neith*, ancient protectress and *'Gateway to the Void.'*

As a visual glyph, the twin tines mounted on a wooden shaft easily suggest a *'horned'* deity, nicknamed for the 'Devil,' 'Old Hornie,' 'Scrat' or 'Hob.' Though there is naturally an element of this potency, present within the Clan Stang, it is clearly one of service to Her. In addition to the cup and knife referred to, we also have the cord and knife, considered by Robert Cochrane to signify the twin pillars of the Mother and Father *either* side of the Cuveen Stang, which is not phallic but represents the now obvious *'Tree of Life.'* Intuition and Intellect again assert themselves as Severity and Mercy, yet also in the cultural traces of Anglo-Saxon binding and bloedisan. It also implies the halter that binds life and the knife that severs it. Fate and Destiny are the one constant in Wyrd. Cochrane hints of this to William Gray where his disdain for the formality of the Kabbalah is clarified in his statement regarding its three pillars as culturally *'alien,'* to his Craft and that he used instead *'an anthropomorphic pattern to shift virtue'* upwards from the ground to the heavens.[128] Moreover, Cochrane considered his 'Faith' to be basically 'feminine,' making cryptic comments about the altar being the *'godstone.'*[129]

Where the Cuveen Stang is placed centrally within the working area emulating the axial pole, geomantic omphalos of the universe, the Paracelsion character of chthonic theory or forces of the *'Stang and Serpent'* are said to open this ring. When placed to the South (Earth), squaring the circle with the staves of the elements, the 'Broom and Lamp' form the bridge that fords the magical tides of manifest causes. But when placed in the North, it becomes the central pillar, flanked by those of the horn (severity) and knife (mercy). North is the place of power, held sacred since draconian times, perceived as the **Gate of Heaven**. Typically the Stang resides here, as primary altar. Cognate with *Daath* as the intermediary and liminal dimension between the Nature of Divinity and the Nature of Man, it represents the time/space continuum of ascent/descent. Purists might argue how the Kabbalah has no place in the Traditional Craft, yet many Kabbalists readily discern concepts cognate with that system. Moreover, Cochrane's own work reflects clear Kabbalistic influence, noted by the eminent (late) Magus William Gray with whom he worked and shared much correspondence.

Conveying more than authority, the Stang wields an archaic power, invested by might representing the supreme 'right' in continuity and perpetuity from inception of awareness of its own absolute status and power (air). It is Godhead and Unity of the Old and Young Horn King as the Supreme altar – Love, Truth and Beauty. The shod foot of the Stang generates Life and Wisdom, the tangs incur Death and Love. From these basic threads there is so much more we may now glean. Representing the hermaphrodite it embodies male and female virtue, wisdom and the third Mystery. The term 'Masking' relates to the symbols placed upon the Stang relative to the rite performed in the form of tools and garlands, and to the actual totem animal mask or skull. These may be mirrored upon the Magister.

In its most *basic* form the 'Mask' represents the four worlds of the Kabbalah, described upon the original basic sketch allegedly drawn by Robert Cochrane. At the base '*Malkuth*' can be seen the serpent, the geomantic force of the Earth. Next, the crossed arrows of '*Yetzirah*' delineate the two opposing triangles of Fire/Air–Male and Water/Earth–Female. When conjoined they superimpose to produce the hexagram *Briah*, the graphic representation of the archaic yab-yum in which the active female mounts the passive male. A crescent Moon cradles a circle of stars, the eight stations of the Sun '*Atziluth*' - the horns of Venus, the master's crown mirrored by the stars of the Zodiacal mantle, of *Nuit* herself. Beyond lies the primal abyss.

Typically, Orthodox Kabbalists will assign the principle masculine gender to *Chockmah* and the principle feminine gender to *Binah*. However, relating this for a moment to astrology, the Zodiacal Best or Girdle of Venus, given as Uranus in *Chockmah* en-souls a feminine potency, generating the masculine quality of Saturn within *Binah*. Yesodic *Malkuth* manifests the *Shekinah* vibration of the Sophianic *Chockmah* or the unredeemed animal soul, our active subconscious known also as the '*nephesch*' or '*psyche*.' This heterodox yet simplistic analysis offers the merest glimpse of its eternal Mysteries that parallels a philosophy correlate with Kabbalistic metaphysics. Charges, chants and prayers evoke the aspect appropriate to the Sabbat upon the Stang as supreme representative of the Horned God, '*Divil*' or Master. The masked and garlanded Stang becomes the

Master of Ceremonies in the North (named by Cochrane as the 'farmer' - Cain, the Father of All) accompanying the Magister's hand-staff.[130]

Looking again at this sketch of the Stang mounted with arrows, a stark graphic is readily discernable of the nine levels of *Yggdrasil*. This expressive narrative is not dependent upon the arcane or historical usage of such symbology, but rather upon intrinsic application of its aesthetic through associative intuition generated by inspiration. Within the nine levels, we have again three trinities or triplicities: the Supernal Triangle of *Kether*, the Crown or 'Father,', the Ethical Triangle of *Chesed, Geburah* and *Tiphareth*, perceived as the 1st 'Son'; the Astral Triangle of *Hod, Yesod* and *Netzach* which is perceived as the 2nd or Tanist 'Son.'[131] The Tree exists in all realms, in all worlds and states of being – hungrily we partake of its 'fruits' as we traverse it from root to crown. Wilfully we choose self-awareness as did Adam and Eve; or gradual detachment. Not as an ascetic, but as a mystic, a seeker of Truth as opposed to illusion. Guidance is offered those who embrace its tripartite nature. For:

"In Fate and the overcoming of Fate, lies the grail."[132]

The Rose emanates from the paradisial *'Tree of Life,'* the body of the Mother, forming the wheel of light (enlightenment) that animates the cross of life the perfumed altar of sacrifices, (carnality and suffering) the juxtaposition of pleasure and pain harmonised within the *Qutub*, or point of Grace. This duality in unity is the phenomenon within the noumenon, the many within the One. Nestled within the central point of every rose is the golden Sun/Son, the flaming spirit of Promethean mysticism. This central golden crown *Kether*, signifies the core Truth of all things. The ten petals of the double rose combine together within the seed unit to represent similar qualities attributed to the eleven Sephiroth (including *Daath*) upon this glorious 'World Tree.' Yet another esoteric example of the mysteries sublimated within symbolic images of nature, especially the cognate forms of the garden, the tree and the maiden. Growing entwined upon the *'Tree of Life,'* the rose clings to and is fed by the Source. The 13th century Sufi mystic and poet Rumi wrote copious odes to the 'eternal beloved' valorising the virtue of the rose. To him, the rose was a 'wise loveliness,' a manifestation of blissful *'fanaa,'* an experience of annihilation of the ego-self and anguish of separation from the Beloved whilst still alive; an illumination that floods the empty soul with Truth (*Pleroma*). He wrote:

> "Like a rose, I smile with all my body, not only with my mouth
> For I am -without myself - alone with the King of the World."[133]

Within Hindu faiths, *'Vac'* is the flaming and illusive 'Word' of Wisdom, the serpentine and unpredictable, mutable winds, expressed as the warrior who staving ignorance, dances amidst Hheaven and Earth, wielding her mighty bow. Again as the *Kharitas*, or Graces, She embodies the tripartite flame of Thought Word and Deed, the flaming *Shin* and Trident staff, the weapon of choice and symbol of divine authority wielded by so many male gods including *Hades, Neptune,* and *Shiva.* Twin pillars are rent to form a cleft, the third ladder of ascent into Her intoxicating gnosis. Emulated often in archaic structures, they were replicated in the pylons of Egypt whose central gateway leads the Pharaoh into the true *'Holy of Holies'* beyond the misty horizon.

It is alleged that these archaic customs were vanquished with the flood, and yet they continue with Abraham, asserting distinctly his tribal god and its symbol the burning bush, a clear cognate of the flaming *'Otz Chim.'* During the Renaissance, Mary Magdalene was referred to esoterically as the *'Burning Bush'* or *'Dryadic Spirit of Life'* by mystics seeking a coterminous reference to the *'Shekinah,'* the tangible presence and fiery breath of God, the Beloved and Genetrix of all wisdom. Tongues of fire represent esoteric principle of divine prophecy, the spiritual fire of inspiration, inflaming the point or person wherein it alights.[134] In fact, the Great Oaks of *Mamre* and *Dodona* were possibly the first trees attributed with the gift of prophecy, imparting inspiration to all who stood beneath their branches. The tongue of the angels, whispering in the winds (known otherwise as glossolalia) becomes the thunderous voice of the mighty gods themselves, finding good example as Inanna's bane within Her much feared and sacred '*Huluppa*' Tree.[135]

Greek legends recount the tale of the Golden Fleece shining with the very beams of the Sun that hung upon the 'Tree of Heaven' for all to witness its glory. Sheltered from their enemies within its massive trunk were the '*Dioscouroi*' the sacred twins Castor and Pollux. In Classical myth two threshold deities noted for their oracular or divinatory gifts, *Diana* and *Janus* to whom the Oak is sacred, find the origin of their names in the root stem for both 'shine/light' and 'go through' signifying 'two' or twice giving us the divine 'twins' who alternately guard the threshold, imparting their reciprocal gift of prophesy.

Other etymologists discern a fortuitous association in Janus/Dianus/Dionysus=light of day rising from two peaks, a clear and unambiguous trinity coterminous with Saturn, Hekate and Hermes, three in one flame of illumination, yet rising still from the Gate of Horn.[136] The Tau letter **T** found in Teutonic *Tius* and Latin *Deus* asserts divinity. Moving further back, Tau formed the stem *tauros*, for bull, the great solar light and Creator. Perhaps this is yet another veiled example of how another facet of the puzzle becomes so easily obscured. She is also the unattainable chaste huntress, he is the all seeing guardian – one still, one movement; one light one dark. It is worth adding here that it is supposed that the species of Oak sacred to Diana is the Holm Oak, a variant not unlike the European Holly, suggesting yet another link with *Dame Holda*.[137]

It is written in the Rig Veda how the '*Celestial Tree of Life*' spans from Hearth to Heaven, guarded unerringly by fantastic winged beasts or birds as personifications of the winds. From its description, it is supposed that it merits as the template for the class of clouds named the '*Trees of Abraham*,' snaring as they do the *fiery* lightning from which soma/amrita or manna is distilled. Imparting knowledge through its vitalising sap, this manifests in poetic and devout inspiration. '*Vac*,' meaning 'pure divine voice,' is the messenger of all Fate or Karma. So we must remember again how, enveloped within the *leafy boughs* of a tree possessed of this blazing virtue, Buddha achieved his 'perfect illumination,' his much sought for enlightenment.[138]

She is cumulatively the Mound, the Pillar, the Monolith, the Tree and all keys to, through and from Her. She is literally the divine source that generates and re-defines its broken branches dripping with manna, the vital elixir and gift of this sacred and holy fiery tree. Dispersed as the legendary '*Golden Bough*,' '*the root and branch of Jesse*,' and the '*tree and root of David*' it has formulated all spiritual bloodlines able to trace their ancestry to Her, and by default the totemic staffs each subsequent leader of that line wields with authority in Her name, be that as Stang or hand-staff/sceptre, from *Tammuz* to *Aeneas* and *Jesse* to *Yeshua*.

Finnish legends similarly recount the Oak tree as the cosmogonical tree, spreading its golden branches across the Heavens. Some scholars therefore conclude the almost indisputable likelihood of a sharing of a root source common to the Semitic and Aryan peoples during the Neolithic.[139] This is surely the origins of the Asclepian rod, the Caduceus of Hermes and other analogous simulacra of Herself as the most sacred and Holy Tree of Naturae, combining the single (measuring) rod (the rule or law of Fate and death), the ring (of life and divine crown or ensign of authority) and the serpent (of wisdom, again indicated by I + O). Moreover, we have the final link herein that concerns the theft of knowledge, wisdom, law etc, all testaments of Fate and faith – the *Mé* held within the 'staff'/'pole' sceptre of Inanna. Stolen and protected by great birds of prey: *Anzu, Ganymede* and *Garuda*, we need only add *Pramantha*[140] (Prometheus) to realise *exactly* the nature of this esoteric Oriflame. Wouldn't that also infer his being the very eagle that tore at his own liver each night, a sacrifice to himself, like the pelican, nourishing its fledglings on its own blood? So too then, the later myth of Christ would conflate that of *Odhin*, sacrificed to himself upon the World Tree for gnosis with the myth of Pelican, whose sacrifice is for others. The eagle is the bird of fire, the supreme aerial symbol of the Sun. It is striking that a great 'eagle' nests within the lofty branches of Yggdrasil, while a 'dragon' (serpent) gnaws at its roots.[141] Another 15th century altar panel illustrates the 'Dream of the Virgin' showing Christ's crucifixion upon a Tree which grows from the womb of the Virgin, his mother. Cresting the Tree, a pelican feeds its young with its own blood, presenting the Grace of Sacrifice. Angels perch on the boughs about him, pensively.[142]

Symbolism stimulates greater insight into mysticism than religion, shunning the dogma that impairs the latter. Curiously, the double trident or Vajra is the equivalent 'staff' of office and distinguishing weapon of the god/s, generating illumination via its diamond flash formed from each of its six horns/points. Again this suggests a connection to the blazing stone of Lucifer: *'Verbum, Lux et Vita'* (Light and Life). Significant twins within classical myth, *'Prometheus'*[143] (forethought/providence) and (hindsight/regret) *'Epimethius'* bear some relevance to the iconic two headed or horned eagle.

As the thunderbird, the thunderer or Zeus, this emblem of the Holy Spirit indicates God's breath. Again the lightning rod becomes a cogent reference in association with the Vajra, the golden bough, the Shaivite trident of Hermes. As death, fire and drought, it is harmonised by life water and storm. So too are the winged or horned *Uraei* indicative of the storm gods of the Middle Eastern Bronze Age, transposing again the transcendence and immanence of air as the power dynamic and superconductor between Earth and the Heavens.

In possible awareness of such currents, assemblies beneath sacred *Gardh* trees entitled 'Things' were held four times a year to 'council' the Clans with advice and share intelligences vital to their harmonious existence. In fact the *'Tree of Life'* is associated with countless mythical poles from the Bi-le tree to the May Pole and from the Stang to Yggdrasil. Crossroads or intersections of contact are frequently described as the *'point of crossing,' 'where three paths meet,'* but better, 'where the *indwelling* god may be raised!' A vital clue here may be confidently associated with the Kundalini, rising snake-like from its coiled state at the base of the sacrum, crossing the metaphysical subtle bodies of *Ida* and *Pingala* through the hypothalamus, the Pearl of *Shiva* to subsume the ego and the superego to the left and right, flooding both hemispheres of the brain with trance inducing hormones.

All green deities draw upon the power of the *Axis Mundi*, the spirit body linked to the 'Crown' via the World Soul, the Great *Shakti* herself. Classical texts describe the dancing by devotees around a tree or pole, believed to house the daimon of a specific, dedicated god. E.J. Jones confirmed this fascinating addendum to me. He asserted that traditional crafters really do dance and process in homage past a seated/enthroned *'Divil.'* And whether beneath a *Gardh* tree or astride a King-stone, He exudes that very evolutionary essence or 'Virtue' promised within the sacred writings that preserve these Truths of Her Wisdom. Initiatory and magical rites may manipulate the Kundalini[144] (though not always) by sexual means to re-align the outer physical, etheric and astral subtle bodies with the inner subtle bodies, the *Ida, Pingala,* and *Sushumna,* fusing a blissful experience of individuation – *"I am He, I am God."* Milton ascribes no less than six gnostic deific virtues to 'Wisdom' as Eternal Providence! These are: Justice; Power; Majesty; Wisdom; Love and Mercy, forming an almost perfect graft for *Yetzirah* the 'Realm of Illusion' under the lunar auspices of *Otz Chim*.

As Sophia She is the adamantine star of Truth, Beauty and Love, coalescing as 'Wisdom'; as Ishtar the Holy Primal Light of Intelligence; and as Wisdom She holds the 'key' to Heaven, with Herself as 'Doorway and Gate.' Her Seal, the pentagram signifies the emotive round of magical ingress through congress and into Her egress. She is the Mother, Teacher and Beloved. As the Shekinah, we are invited to explore Truth, Love and Beauty through the lens of Her glorious reflection here on Earth, the divine *'Madre dei'* borne of the divine Wisdom - *Achamoth* of *Chokmah*. Moreover, as the *'Stella Maris,'* the mournful light over the waters, Her spirit is the primal Mem, the Void of all courses and causes. In one of the Nag Hammadi texts entitled *'On the Origin of the World'*, Adam kneels before Eve, calling her the Mother of all living, announcing it was She who gave him life.[145]

In Ophite traditions we see reflected the allied mystic premise of the cosmological emanations of Light, Thought and Word from the Unmanifest Negative Veils of the Void, and how this single act of Beauty then became manifest through refraction via seven intelligences or potencies of the celestial realms. These in turn are linked via a complex matrix of correspondences to mankind, the created form of these forces. The Triune Stang of the Order of the Sun asserts this assignment in addition to the Classical elements of Fire, Water and Air. Of course even as all of these are placed obviously upon *Otz Chim*, they are less easily read upon the Stang. Earth especially sets the foot within the manifest plane serving as the platform of ascent via its symbolic and idiosyncratic narrative.

Wherever two kings, genii or rampant beasts flank a third potency between, it is almost certainly always a tree, figuratively or literally, exampled in stunning bas-reliefs, sculptures and friezes across the ancient world from Asia to Akkad, and Greece to Phoenicia. Magnificent wall plaques taken from Assyrian temples circa 700BCE depict two winged spirits libating the *'Tree of Life.'* When in Purgatory, Dante marvelled at the *'Inverted Tree'* so designed, he felt that ascent was impossible without a chariot. Plato certainly expressed his profound understanding of mankind as a celestial plant, in other words, an *'Inverted Tree'* whose roots draw 'Ruach' downwards from the Heavens, along the branches as they reach deep into the Earth below. Wisdom is the sap that feeds the mystic whence the vehicle of Faith lifts the soul towards the light of Truth – a *'Waking to Omniscience.'* This whispering Sentinel of the Sun becomes the *'Horse of Agni, Lord of the Trees,'* (*Vanaspati*) the **fiery** omphalos and igneous heart of the arboreal axial pole of *Brahma*:

> "Root above, branches below: this primal fig-tree!
> Pure indeed is its root: it is Brahman, known as the Immortal.
> In it rests all the worlds: No-one so ever goes beyond it.
> *All this, verily, is that tree."*[146]

Later Kabbalistic cosmology similarly describes the 'Tree' as descending *from above*. This demands the climb by faith and belief back to the pure source:

> "Happy is that portion of Israel, in whom the Holy One, blessed be He, delights and to whom He gave the Torah of Truth, the Tree of Life, Who so ever takes hold of this achieves life in this

World and in the World to come. Now the Tree of Life extends from downward, and is the Sun which illumines all."[147]

In fact a moments study of the divine 'Hexagram' or the conjunction of *Shiva* and *Shakti*, reveals how the dynamic of the two ternaries of three radiant male fiery kalas and three fluid female watery kalas revolve around a 7th Tipharetic qutub of ascent and descent distinguished as the *'Eye of the World'* – *'Janua Coeli'* and doorway of Heaven. *Dionysus* is the Gorgon Mask of God, formed of the Primordial Trinity, the generative prismic spark between *Shakti* and *Shiva*, who as the 'twin' terminates *Metatron*[148] and *Sandalphon* assume the visage of *'Malakh'* - shadows of divine madness (reflective emanations) that diffuse illuminatory gnosis via the epiphanic bridge at the point of rapture.

Dionysus' brutal Thyrsus morphs into the Caduceus of *Apollo*; vigour and logic, the dark and bright twins snake upwards in ascent towards the crowning pinnacle to the unseen presence of the Star between the tines. Celestial twins emanate the qualities of light and dark and the cusp between them. Shin is the glyph for this primal fire, depicted artistically as the tri-lobed Iris or Lily. Poetically, this is seen in the Awen and the triskele among others, giving us the final and most profound realisation of the Stang – of who and what it is.

Three axial spheres rotate without motion exuding vibrational kalas that pervade our three states of consciousness. This map of the Universe relates to states of sentience, representing the key to experiential noumena and phenomena. Typical of many European cultures, a trinity becomes defined by a synthesis of thesis and anti-thesis, the Tanist kingship of complimentary not conflicting virtue. Here the triune 'Mother' is again attended by dual suitors to express the divine cosmogony, symbolised by this one Stang, the composite of so many variants of the underlying Mythos relevant to so many cultures.

Cochrane refers to the 'Three Mothers' reflected in the Oak, Ash and (black) Thorn trees possessing the Virtue of the Pale, the Fecund and the Dark One, again embodied in the three worlds of Inanna's *Huluppa Tree*: the Seas, the Earth and the Heavens.[149] These potencies and correspondences find another amazing parallel as noted by Robert Cochrane in Taliesin's *'Song of Amergin,'* a spell binding chant invoking the Virtue of the seas, the Earth and the skies until all become suffused as 'fire' in the head. Cochrane describes the formulae in terms of an authentic attainment of transcendence, and as 'high code.'[150]

We may safely conclude with Cochrane's assertion of Woman (as Maid) as the reflux of the World Soul (*Shekinah*) in whom Virtue becomes the binding rhythm and evolutionary force of Her Clan to the *Axis Mundi* and *Anima Mundi*. The Stang she embodies represents possession of this Virtue.[151] Within the Mysteries of Abraxas is a fascinating reference to the seven fold 'Rose of Flame' expressed as the (Spiritus) breath or 'World Soul,' where as Sophia, she manifests as the Shekinah, and is both cognate and relevant to fiery Jinn.[152]

In Tantra, there are spiritual entities totalling 24[153] that are again reflected within the Clan's Wind Rose, the Compass of Aetts, presiding over its four cardinal and four intermediate points. Of the runic alphabet, it is simply another expression of the 24 winds that circumvent the nine worlds. The *'Odel'* glyph, cognate with the Greek omega, infers the right of inheritance through the Clan guardian or Egregore in modern parlance. This force of virtue becomes 'attached' to the head of the Clan, imparting knowledge and protection to all under its aegis.[154] In Teutonic lore, twenty-four Valkyries ride as the winds...headed by the beautiful and terrible pale–faced Frau Gaude, who fiercely nurtures and chides Her children. This protective spirit of wisdom is easily cognate with Ishtar, the Gate of Heaven and Earth as the house or '*Womb of the Fish,*' the spirit of resurrection and of the Holy Spirit if light and life – the *Luz*!

"To open the lock of Heaven, belongs to my supremacy" declaims Ishtar.

As spiritual forces, both the Shekinah and the Valkyrie join Her as expressions of the 'Tutelary Source' of the generative Virtue of divinity for those peoples under the aegis of their named god/s. This rune further serves as 'bond' for the 'people' and between the people and their God. Odel presents itself to the psyche as the fish, the yoni gateway stimulating cerebral fusion as we trace it into alternate realities, swimming across the Great Sea of Marah in search of the intuitive current (*neschemah*) that will lead us towards the Source thereto grasp the promised wisdom gnosis, or Grail heritage of the Fisher King. It serves as the mediating portal between two planes, the Vesica Piscis and hypnogogic rainbow bridge that generates a balanced state or true twilight of *'antahkarana.'* This is where:

"the hunter, Old Tubal Cain and the Roebuck in the thicket are both one and the same divine presence."[155]

Within these sublime mysteries of sacrifice upon the '*altar of perfumes,*' a pattern emerges, witnessed in the deceptively simple glyph for the Stang, each point of which serves the multi-faceted genius of a strikingly universal yet markedly unique cosmology, finding expression and expansion through archaic myth, itself nourished by the psychic formulae hardwired into our cellular matrix. And so, as it was in the beginning, and will be until the end, '*Asherah*' is within our sight and our grasp. She is after all the journey to *Caer Sidi*, the *Castle Dolorous* and *Caer Ochren*, and the Hill upon which they stand; all is within and without the abode of the divine She, the Bright, Pale, and Dark Goddess of Life, but also of Death and Wisdom.

"Hail, Star of the Sea! God's gracious Mother,
Thou happy Gate of Heaven.
O Lady most glorious, Exalted above the heavens;
Thou art become the window of heaven.
Tis thou that art the gate of the King on high,
And of bright light portal art thou."[56]

The 4th Nail

"Time is Father to the Queen of Truth"[157]

Etruscan society venerated its women. In contra-distinction to the virulent andro-centrism of Greek and later Roman cultures the women of Etruria were the single most prominent focus for art, mythology and religious iconography. Many beautiful artefacts and ritual impedimenta depict a natural style, devoid of the rigid formality of their misogynistic counterparts. Though, because of this pronounced gender bias, it is difficult to assume correlates among their respective pantheons. Curiously, because the Etruscans had almost exactly the same number of deities as they had (consonant) letters of an alphabet; academic opinion asserts it to be a Greek derivative. And yet, the Etruscans deified each letter, through its sound – phonetics! The breath, or aspirative invocation of the gods, manifest as the Word. To this society more than most, everything sacred had a symbol, and each symbol was deemed to have inherent virtue.

An ornate bronze speculum circa 320BCE, typical of many, depicts cameo scenes pertinent to Etruscan mythology. This particular mirror relates the tragedy of Time, where human subjectivity in its regard enforces particular courses of predictable action, known commonly as 'cause and effect.' Gloomily unavoidable – it is always a 'matter of course' before 'Time' meters its own force, bringing it to bear within the manifest world, pronouncing the reality of the 4th dimension upon the other composite three required for us to register the imperative that:

> '...space-time is four dimensional because the location of a point in 'Time' is independent of its location in space.'[158]

Illustrated within the bronze ornamentation are doomed lovers that hereon in become subject to a 'Fate' no longer forestalled, as the irate heroine wreaks vengeance upon those she once protected. A geis-laden object re-emerges as the foci as and for the precise 'moment in time' upon which 'effect' hinges upon 'cause.' The three dimensions here that brought Time into play were the choices made subject to the interplay of 'Fate' upon circumstance.

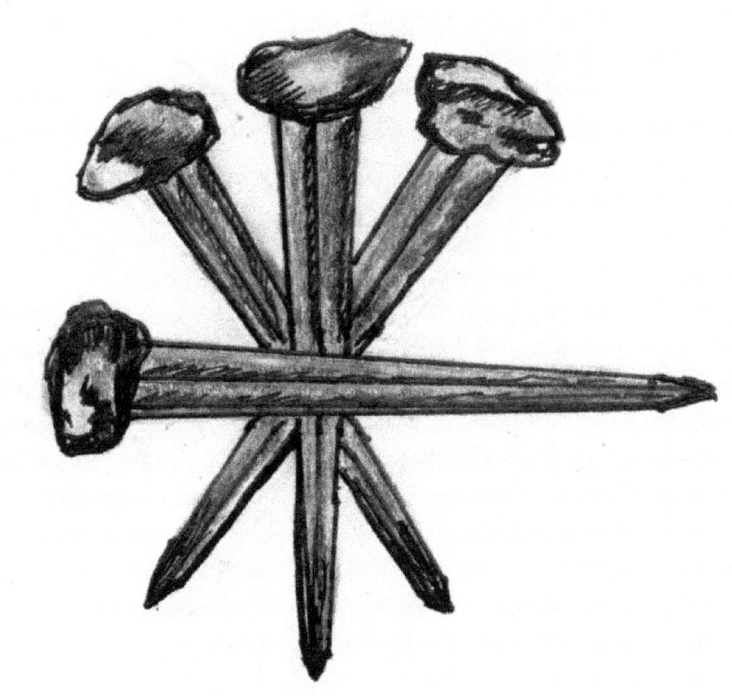

Four Nails

'Three coordinate axes are given, each perpendicular to the other two at the origin, the point at which they cross.'[159]

The instrument of deliverance is a beautiful winged Goddess named *Athrpa* (often, and I believe erroneously associated with the Greek *Atropos*) who, wielding a hammer in her right hand (cause/action) and a long nail in her left hand (effect/justice), secures the 'point' of impact by her ambivalent act of driving home this nail, anchoring it at a nodal crossroads upon this web of human interchange.

Winged figures, popular within early Christian art and later Victorian romanticism, find their origin within these stylized examples of Etruscan art.[160] Several of their many deities became conflated when Olympia required only twelve gods to represent the Roman pantheon. Study of these led me to recognize another female deity aspected within *Athrpa*; she is Dame Fate identical in this respect to *'Turan,'* a true Etruscan correlate of the Greek Aphrodite who morphs somewhat uncomfortably into the Roman Venus, becoming sadly diminished as a rather vacuous 'mother' of the home. The Hindu Goddess of abundance and life, named *'Shri Maha Lakshmi,'* again, like Aphrodite, is similarly born of the foamy waters, being propitiated for favourable enterprise, affirming further links between Fate, beauty and water. Noteworthy here is the fourth face of Brahma, believed by practitioners of Kaula Tantra to symbolize the fourth ventricle of the brain, cogently stimulated by the risen Kundalini. Within the 'Compass,' the Triune path of the Tau becomes the Fourth pathway of the Crossroads, approached through Trance Mediumship – an awareness that breaches the actuation of Time.

Within our literal world however, we are subject to mundane elementals, and of spatial awareness beyond which the aegis of Time advances the field of exploration into the 4th dimensional metaphysical force as the sole province of *'Dame Fate,'* un-manipulated as yet by man.

Time is the axis of spin, the freedom from stasis. Even so, it is judged harshly by those who undervalue its true worth and fail to recognize its full potential.

> 'A temporal dimension is a dimension of Time. Time is often referred to as the "fourth dimension" for this reason, but that is not to imply that it is a spatial dimension. A temporal dimension is one way to measure physical change. It is perceived differently from the three spatial dimensions in that there is only one of it, and that we cannot move freely in time but subjectively move in one direction.'[161]

As mere human beings, subject to the laws of physics at play upon our manifest realm we hold three nails only, these being the triangulation points of our personal geography, wherein we are the unique centre of our own universe. Such a position reveals our will, our purpose – our 'point' if you like, for being there. To this 'point,' Time asserts the 4th principle of non-spacial dynamics, honing who, what and where we are, to 'why.' That is to say, whatever lineage/descent any of us accrue, our survival and return to and through that nourishing stream of individual and collective evolution is within Her remit, subject to and in accord with *our will* by Her (right) hammer and as Cause to *Her Divine Will* to effect Her (left) nail; all choice is attained though lateral application of 'free will' where 'Fate' alone controls the elements and constraints of 'Time' offered to us.

She instigates the prime moments for our epiphanies, our trials, our euphoria, birth and eventual death. Engagement, knowingly in this process facilitates our becoming, wandering as children of Cain upon the path where destiny poises, awaiting our claim. Along that path, we search in earnest for Her 4th nail, forged at the dawn of our making, irrevocably sealing our destiny through and by its point of leverage and anchorage.

That is, until we are finally able to recognize the purpose in its existence, and thus realize and overcome by immersion, our ability to achieve our destiny where being:

> 'In Fate,' allows us to 'overcome fate' in order then to grasp at last, 'the Grail.'[162]

It is at this moment we see and recognize the 4th Nail, the instrument of Fate, by its mastery we may seize the day, thus realizing the destiny of our birthright. This recognition is no less than an epiphany of our own divinity depicted obtusely in the Sumerian cuneiform script where the glyph for virtue/essence of the divine or anything possessed of it (*ilu*) is the '*Dingr.*' Composed of four strokes, three fanned uprights (rather like a stylized fleur de lys) crossed in the centre by the fourth, horizontally. Essentially the three determine the manifest causalities, the fourth crossed nail seals, defines and closes them. The Three Mothers (of Fate) wield the fourth strike of the 'Father' who as Time, draws all to a close, to that single point. Of the Fabled Horsemen of the Apocalypse, it is of course the Fourth Pale Rider, who as Death marks that point of egress.

As the three-fold Creatrix and World Soul, She has the power to unify, connect and direct the heavenly and earthly causalities into an harmonic fruition. Hekate wields this authority though She was once an obscure goddess among countless others adopted by the Greeks, She bears a remarkable likeness not just to *Athrpa*, but also to *Vanth*, the winged psychopompic figure who likewise wields a key, a serpent and a flaming torch! Hekate is commonly depicted with three faces, where logic dictates the presence of a fourth, albeit one that is 'hidden.' Through gnosis gained under the direction of Her Three Faces, the fourth face is finally revealed to us. From this Crossroads Qutub the potentialities of ingress generates congress; and if congress is correctly engaged through the right choices whence offered, we may then aspire to egress, to gloam the enigmatic veil of Her 4th face – realized as *'kairos,'* or 'God's own Time.'

As Mistress of Fate, She is able to distinguish the quality of time from eternity, night from day and the Heavens from the Earth; Her rhythmic dance is the harmonic friction of becoming and overcoming in perpetuity. Purposefully, She wields the tools of Her trade - the Hammer and Nail forged by *Sethlans* (exemplary variant of Tubal Cain) the Etruscan God of fire and the forge to mark Time and Tide, to 'fix' them as the manifest expression of Her Will.[163] At this axial moment, Wisdom asserts itself in that vital point of crossing, the singular moment of 'now,' an aspect of verifiable 'Truth' as fleeting as it is rare.

Yet the mystery of Time as a manifest law has suffered adversely under patristic oligarchies. Is 'Father' Time not in fact Her 4th Face, the one that separates Her from eternity, who as wisdom asserts manifest form through Norea, the 4th child of Adam and daughter of Eve? An Anglo-Saxon Blessing hints at the identity of the *fourth* being a feminine, wisdom Virtue akin to Norea in Frigg, the Aesir wife and mother to the Gods, in " Flags, Flax, Fodder and *Frigg!*" Frigg subsumed the role of an earlier Germanic goddess of the Earth, named Nerthus, whose worship according to Tacitus, took place in sacred groves. Her name is also cognate with Gaude/Gode/, later Hilde/Holda and oddly also with Bertcha – the White (pale) Lady who rides out from the Mound to lead the Wild Hunt. Mistress of the Winds, prophecy and collector of souls, she harvests the fallen *'gathering in her children that she might take us home again.'*

Three pillars of Strength, Beauty and Wisdom become the Awen or manifest potencies executed through the *'Three Rings.'* They also become the *'Three Nails,'* or more properly, the Three Ladies of *'Fate'* within folklore more familiar to many. Within the axial centre asserted by the Stang as the celestial Nux and hub of the Nowl star (Alpha Polaris), it becomes the Tau, whose three arms or paths focalize the self 'immolation' that manifests the fourth path - the 4th 'Nail' of *Time!* In fact, Polaris is described by gypsy folk-lore as being the iron 'point' of destiny, the fourth nail about which the mill of Time circuits the Heavens, forged by the elder gods when mankind was in its infancy.

Within the 'Mysteries of Britain,' Lewis Spence refers to the Earth as '*Three Queens,*' the seasonal sister spouses of (another fine example of male oriented bias in) Arthur, the Archer.[164] However, in the Rig Veda, '*Vac*' the divine breath as Wisdom, is said to 'dance' amidst the Heaven and Earth, wielding Her Bow of *Truth*. S/he is 'Time and Tide' to 'Fate.' S/he is the instrument through which Her Will is executed; Hers is the force here given Form and whether as Hammer or Bow, the dart and nail pierce the Illusion of Life. And again in a document ascribed to Robert Cochrane is echoed this visionary sentiment with regard to Creation:

> "there is a great river flowing and twining round all creation, rushing out of Annwn, binding the seven kingdoms together, and returning to Annwn in a great waterfall, under which all must pass eventually. The name of that river is Time and the place of Darkness to which it returns is not only Hell, but Heaven also. It is Time and Time alone that binds us to blindness, and it is love and love alone that will let us see the golden heart of the Mysteries."[165]

Remembering that the plane of transformation is the Earth itself, the aforementioned 'Four Queens' temper the 'Hamitic' descendents of Cain, the original '*wanderer*' whose Fate, in consigning him to the Moon engenders our mindful engagement to evolve beyond the subjective constraints of 'Time,' beyond the bounds of it and beyond the purpose of it.[166] But isn't that precisely why 'Time' has no place within the 'Ring of Arte' and why we say that the Mysteries are Eternal! The bounds we set about ourselves are there to ensure we stave the Hand of Fate, until we are ready to offer the knowing heart to the piercing of Her nail - the 4th nail, subject to that precise and blissful 'point' of 'Time,' in the Beloved, in *'Kairos'*?

> "And if your eyes cannot fix on the real reality, I will always guide them, so that your eyes turn not aside, nor exceed the limit of Truth. And I will surround you with a glow, and in that light you will see My Beauty everywhere. And you will have such quietude that you may always hear what I say. And I will teach you the language of the soul, which will make you comprehend the mystery of your being lifted to Me, and the wisdom of our meeting." (Ibn 'Arabi)

Dark Aegipan and Pale Leukothea

"Ineffable, hidden, brilliant scion, whose motion is whirring, you scattered the dark mist that lay before your eyes and, flapping your wings, you whirled about, and through this world you brought pure light." Orphic Hymn to Phanes.

Vainglorious divine satyr, lusty and merciless. Pan is the magnificent Goat-Foot God! Yet despite popular descriptions that too often refer to Pan as the great and lusty satyr, originally he was never so. Believed to hail from Thrace, he is also too often perceived as the Old Horned Nature God. But this proto-shamanic entity had evolved from the Sumerian Goat-Fish God of land and sea – Enki, archaic benefactor of all humankind, a nurturing and evolutionary deity. Haunting the wild and lonely hills and mounds, this titanic god exhibits chthonic aspects and is another form or derivative of the dark 'Goat of Mendes.' From Chaos, he fashions life. His divine manifestation unites life and spirit as absolute perfection – beast and angel combined to formulate humankind.

Drawing virtue (power) from the New Moon, he wanders Arcadia alone and brooding, reflecting deeply upon his 'Cain-like' status. This wild and hairy Woodwose, hermit and wanderer at some point became aligned to this Lunar Sphere, illuminated within the heavens. Throughout ancient Greece, commemorative races were held in Pan's honour of his high status within the mysteries; as a significant deity he was celebrated in festivals for the dead along with Hermes and Artemis. Torch-bearers held vigil for the gift of fire, a defiant element of wisdom gnosis from Prometheus – forethought, or first thought, Pan in fact!

Pan's increasing association with light and sacred fire became reflected in his names: 'Phanos' by the Greeks and 'Lucidus' by the Romans, both of which describe the brightness of a shining light, a holy effulgence linking him firmly through Orphism, with Phanes, god of 'light'. Yet his presence is said to induce 'pan-ic', an awe filled loss of calm that generates a surging rush of adrenalin, a thrill likened to the *petit mort* a sexual rousing, deep and primal. Such blatant responses have forged links between Pan and Azazel and also to Saturn, ruler of the goat of Capricorn, who is often portrayed as a winged serpent. Chronos is similarly depicted in this form of the Orphic seraph, being a composite of an eagle (Water/Scorpio), a bull (Earth/Taurus) and a lion (Fire/Leo), together with the face of a man/god (Air/Aquarius), depicting the Four Cardinal Winds that also parallel the four beasts and throne angels of the later apostles collectively.

Called Protogonos (First-Born) and Eros (Love), Phanes generated the seed of gods and men. Phanes, for shine and light, signifies he who acts as, or who facilitates, ie: 'Manifestor' or 'Revealer'. Phanes within Hesiod's 'Theogony' (the birth or story of the gods) is described in the cosmic beginning along with Khaos (Air) and Gaia (Earth). Phanes, like Janus, is sometimes depicted with two faces; one fore and one aft - forethought and afterthought, the dual attributes of Prometheus and his tanist brother Epimetheus.

Phanes Protogonos, born of the Cosmic Egg, most probably a meteorite, a flaming ball of light that falls to Earth, is described as luminous and radiant; a polymorphic god of the mysteries with glittering wings and cloven hooves, manifest perfection of primal and celestial form.

Occasionally this aeonic character is depicted as androgynous. Controlling stars, lightening and all celestial luminaries, both Pan and Phanes are placed central to a zodiac mandorla representing the passage of time through the eternal Cosmos, whose wisdoms we may draw upon from this ancient and mystical Patron.

Notably, Pan, in no way a simple rural deity, did not live among the other gods of Olympus away from their creation, but among humankind, a pastoral shepherd and imminent guide to his flocks. Sometimes, Phanes is given triune qualities, presiding as a triple god of all fire, all light: the light giver, the light of life and the light of love, symbolising the magical forces we may harness of Will, Action and Wisdom.

It is relevant that we may review history as a sequence of three mythological ages. The first Titanic Age ruled by Chronos/Saturn; the second Silver Age by Zeus/Jupiter and the third Golden Age by Phanes/Sun. Seraphic Phanes, born of the Mystic Egg, bound by the winged Ouroboros, 'father' of all gods and all men, is frequently linked to Helios, Eros, Zeus and Dionysus in addition to Pan. In Arcadian myth, the Sun named *Uz*', is a synonym for goat. As a star, the goat can be seen rising and setting, particularly at the Winter Solstice, during the residence of the Sun in Capricorn – house of the goat!

Interestingly, the Greek word for 'Tragedy' finds its stem root in the word meaning 'goat', for this was the animal that consumed and ravaged the vine, sacred to Dionysus, hence the goat became the prime sacrifice to this god of festival, theatre and ritual. Drama itself began as sacred dancing rites held in honour of Dionysus, and means simply the 'act of,' or 'doing of'; meaning the holding of His sacred Rites. Contra to this the Comedic mask was developed from the concept within 'comedy' of farce and revelry under the guise of religious duty through humour, and its release through 'acts' of 'playing the goat'. These vital clues afford us a lateral, insightful perspective into sacred 'Drama' where rites honoured the roles of gods and Fate within the lives of humankind, here upon Earth. Tragic tales of heroes and hubris roused all spectators into wild and frenzied release, a cathartic participation that brought them closer to their gods. Originally, an amphitheatre was a holy place housing an altar upon which sacrifices were made to those gods being celebrated and worshipped in the religious rites held there.

Returning now to Pan/Phanes, within the Zohar, we may read how the 'Holy One' rises at midnight, journeying to the 'garden' to converse with the 'Righteous Ones'. During the solstices and equinoxes, all accusation (from the 'satans') shall cease, again only at this appointed moment, the luminal threshold between states and zones of light and time. Only at midnight is the equilibrium of force and form and all opposites possible. This suggests something really quite phenomenal and very intriguing. Just consider how in that threshold moment, which is technically an eternity, everyone and everything is exonerated, all is made pure, all is granted the universal wisdoms and all polarities become resolved within the third state of being; the Crowned Hermaphrodite becomes a reality. And thus is Pan the gateway, the key, the light and leader to this accomplishment. Pan is the form of the boundary and the force to transcend it.

Conversely, in folklore, it is said that 'he who casts no shadow is Pan,' who resting at noon, creates the still point, both in the Cauldron, which is generally said to be ever churning, and the Sun within the macrocosmic heavens above – another conjunction of the shadow and the bestial form of man/goat, where both become 'as one.' It is a common mistake to conflate him with Priapus, the ithyphallic god of fertility and agriculture; Pan is lord of the pastoral Earth, of the eternal Arcadia, idyllic land of the gods and heroes all. Aegipan is the epithet given to this illustrious figure, seen as the saviour of the Greeks in their adversity, a crisis of evolution and a nostalgic desire for a life less complex during a time when only three seasons ruled the calendar. Autumn is a more modern construct that obfuscates the triune nature of life, religion, God and the Cosmos. The Caduceus, staff of Hermes, of the pilgrim and herald to the gods is the single staff or mace, the sceptre of the ambassador, pole of office, carrying the authority of the god it serves. It is the staff of the nightmare, of fevers and night sweats, linking the hunter to the shepherd, the sacrificer to the sacrificed.

The scapegoat is the chosen beast, burdened with the aegis of a people whose purification depends upon its sacrifice. Often a criminal was chosen, dressed and arrayed in green leaves and robes to 'act the goat' for the sacred drama – the rites of appeal to the 'all god' – the Aegipan! Love and death embrace Fate, the final liberator and primal genetrix to whom the intoxicating divine madness subsumes within the kinetic act of release, the ecstasy of assimilation, of sublime frenzy as the shift presents union within the 'One.' Green Dionysus, drunken Dionysus bears the 'mask of God' the bridge between all realms. Madness is the device of change, the mark of progress, the catalyst for true evolution, fighting stagnation where logic drowns the voice of freedom.

Pan guards the original sacred grove in Arcadia. Reared on the milk of Amaltheia, sacred She-Goat and wet-nurse to the gods, Pan attains wisdom, docility and the propensity towards impetuous violence. From the mountains to the caverns within them, the Sophianic goddess of Parnassus, commonly known through Her construct as the Muse, meticulously and succinctly performs and reads the oracles and divinations which are then gifted to humanity. Apollo 'usurps' from Pan these arts of Prophecy. Perhaps, however, 'usurps' in this instance is more likely a euphemism for the 'continuity' from the Old Horned, Woodwose and

Celestial Wanderer to the Solar and more sedentary officiating temple, where the Muse may openly be acknowledged. Pan's horned Thyrsus, his brutal and primal staff, symbolising blood, death, life and sacrifice is better suggested as a 'gift' to Apollo; through Hermes. This staff acquires the spun serpent, ever present symbol of oracular wisdom and of the chthonic potencies of Hermes and Hekate.

Seven strings to the lyre and seven reeds to Pan's love-lorn syrinx; both are instruments of sublime music, the second of three arts of civilisation. The first being agriculture, expansion and war (Truth). The second is song, music and dance (Beauty). The third is belief, faith and mysticism [Love]. All became subsumed within the bright and shining Apollo, bearer of the East Wind, who 'seized' the Oracle at Delphi, killing the python (Pan-Hermes), his dark twin and North Wind. Once he had removed the 'head' of the 'serpent' it became the bone oracle, the speaking skull, Baphomet, the Baptist and Bran – Devil's head, sporting the Horns of wisdom upon his 'blazing' brow! In the Mound of Delphi, this serpent/python did once reside, Grendel-like, within.

Looking into the etymology of Pan, we discover the word: 'paein' meaning to pasture in terms of (pastoral) care, governing the land, flocks, farmers, fishermen and hunters. He is the 'upright man,' the goatherd and shepherd, the sacrifice and the sacrificed. He is innovation and the innovator. Typhon, the poisonous scorching wind from the South is the nightmare, the harbinger of bad dreams and ill-tempers/humours.

Pan the Goat-Foot God, to become lover to the beautiful Pale Moon Goddess, changed into a stunning ram. To commemorate this fecund act, each year the priests of Pan, the *'Lupercai'* protect their territory, beating the bounds, driving off all evil spirits/humours, shrieking and striking their slim animal hide 'whips' into the air and upon any woman of a fertile age in arm's reach. Pan is thus *'Drighton,'* the ancient overlord,

'Providence,' the reciprocal and obligatory protector, provider and mentor: the three-fold innovator of humankind, on Earth, sea and shore. Invoked into the central fire, the hearth of every abode, He is the celestial and superior goat. Pan, all god, is truly god of all.

Pan's three 'sisters' according to some original sources are the *'Parcae,'* the triple godmothers who grant three boons upon birth, marriage and death, the three Graces who charmingly assist Pan to execute his innovative arts. Cognate with Pan, Hermes also protects flocks and travellers, yet bears the Ram as his totem. Through his Roman equivalent, the ancestral tutelary spirits are known as 'Sons of Mercury.'

According to Pausanias, *Leukothea* was, after Hermes and Poseidon, the most celebrated and honoured goddess in and around ancient 'Korinth.' She was a dedicated 'Bacchant' and some say the wet nurse and surrogate mother to Dionysus, the 'Star-Child.' The Mater Matuta, Pale-Faced Goddess of the seas, sailors and storms asserts a coterminous link through Poseidon with the tragic Nereid, *Leukothea* (the once human, Ino, deified after her own sacrificial apotheosis). She is the Light and Fire of the Dawn and of the East, bringing gnosis and wisdom to her wards. Pan shares the responsibilities and duties of a true patron of the land and seas. Her warding hand of five points is Her shield and focus against all sea frets and storms, calming the waters until serene. Protected under the aegis and patronage of Poseidon, she in turn protects those dedicated to Her. Aphrodite of the Sea, the Stellar Maris, stretches forth Her benedictions to become the compassionate Lady of Grace.

Hail Mary!
"To Leukothea, Fumigation from Aromatics.
I call, Leukothea, of great Kadmos born, and Dionysos' nurse, who ivy leaves adorn.
Hear, powerful Goddess, in the mighty deep vast-bosomed,

destined thy domain to keep: in waves rejoicing, guardian of mankind; for ships from thee alone deliverance find, amidst the fury of the unstable main, when art no more avails, and strength is vain.

When rushing billows with tempestuous ire overwhelm the mariner in ruin dire, thou hearest with pity touched his suppliant prayer, resolved his life to succour and to spare.

Be ever present, Goddess! In distress, waft ships along with prosperous success: thy mystics through the stormy sea defend, and safe conduct them to their destined end."

Orphic Hymn 74 to Leukothea (trans. Taylor) (Greek hymns C3rd B.C. to 2nd A.D.)

Cain and Craft Diversity

"The Patriarchal Societies of the Three Desert Tribes of the Middle East, and their fragmented descendants, have never had a cosmology that allowed for a unity and relationship between life forms and the planet. Instead, they view the human species as the crowning achievement of Creation, the manifestation (albeit flawed), of the Creator. These views are the antithesis of tribal thought and arrogantly seek to fragment, compartmentalize, and subjugate life rather than recognizing the universe as a single interrelated, interdependent entity. Instead of relying on a context of relationship and co-dependence to find one's place, civilized men place distinctions on separate events, and each of their thoughts exist independently and separate from the whole."[167]

The Craft encompasses many modes of practice, all of which reflect the variant needs and attainments of its adherents. To use a simple analogy: a person who is to all intents and purposes a good, moral and charitable person who may never attend their cultural place of worship is no less a member of that Faith than the ascetic or holy man/woman who devotes every moment to prayer. None is superior to the other; the difference between them is merely one of spiritual aspiration.

Similarly, possessing various 'magical' tools or a vast collection of spells or charms, no matter how old, does not qualify you as Magus or worker of magics, any more than owning a set of recipes makes you a cook. Only the knowledge of how they work and the skills of application will coax fruition. People within the Craft draw upon and develop the 6th sense, linking the noumenal world to the phenomenal. Sadly the Craft also attracts many sensationalists and charlatans where such parasites drain the life-blood from the very source that nourishes it.

In my short term as a writer, I have been sharply and quite unfairly confronted for my profound descriptions of the 'Black Goddess,' labelled anti-feminist for my promotion of male deity and elitist for my uncommon view of both! Which not only proves that people never thank you for honest yet challenging views as pathways to the Truth, but that you really cannot ever do is please all of the people all of the time; nor must we try. This decent into madness is the lapwing that distracts us from our true course. And so we must choose our words carefully whether spoken or written to convey an absolute purpose, distinguishing between religion and spirituality, magical and occult, wisdom and knowledge, power and force, matter and form, pagan and witch. It is often said that the meaning of a word lies within its use, if so, then it 'becomes' in the sense of its implication rather than its representation.

Being elitist is not a divine trait, but a human one. That mankind has for millennia fashioned his Gods in likeness of himself is a tragic truism, yet the God's elude such limiting definitions. These illusions are mere conduits for a Source that is pure, untainted by human corruption. Its forces of khaos and destruction are not guided by choice or preference. Nor are they so by greed nor power mongering. All is balance, a natural intelligent design. We can choose to scrabble along in our sectarian dogmas practising superstitious primitive magics or we can embrace the science, the logic, the ecstasy of freedom within absolute sentience.

In speculating the nature of deity Philo the Jew aptly said:

> "true knowledge is to recognize our ignorance - all that we know of God is that we do not know him at all."

All we can do is make relative statements. However, if we accept that deity is both immanent and transcendent, that is both within and without both spirit and matter, then we have to also finally concede that there is no dualism or polarity, a unity - no more, no less - the final Mystery, the revelation of the hidden, the dark light within the light -the ultimate paradox, a Truth beyond all comprehension.

So where and how does all of this affect our modern practise of the Craft?

Traditionalists are frequently described as 'dual faith' because our deities can easily be recognised within those of mainstream religions that have been appropriated and overlaid with those own cosmologies. Those within the Traditional Craft could for example, freely enter any place of worship, be it a church, temple or synagogue, to pray and propitiate a working…..this would be construed as a legitimate rite. Here there is another clear distinction with Paganism. Throughout Western history, witchcraft was seen as a syncretism of Christian ideas based around pagan religious concepts; hence the survival of so many pagan and folk superstitions relating to protection against malignant acts.

Extraordinarily, the earliest records from the 4th millennium BCE reveal no distinct deity for either malignant (cursing) or benevolent (blessing) acts of magic. In fact, the same (ambivalent) god was petitioned for both. Separation occurred only after Zoroastrian dualism around 600BCE entered Judaism and thus by default, Christianity and Islam, irrevocably corrupting the whole Western idioms of magic and witchcraft. Any deity could be petitioned for assistance, but usually a tribal/city/ tutelary god would be deemed better suited to consider the worthiness of each case. Ironically, counter magic by the recipient or victim would have been made to the same deity - both sides were judged on merit/ intent/ sincerity. Moreover, the same term was used for invoking the power or force modern practitioners would deem 'good' or 'evil' spirits; in fact it is only the *intent* that defines purpose. The outcome rested entirely with the petitioned god who then determined the success or failure of the magics cast. Requests were normatively for all perceived evil to be returned to the sender. Malicious acts were therefore considered illegal, counter magic was, however, quite legitimate!

During this period the Gods were perceived as the heavenly 'judges.' All rites were constructed as speeches for defence or prosecution. Rituals such as these were designed as trials, where the Gods acted as jurors affecting the outcome; it was their power alone, not man's that governed the state of play - this was the vital distinction. It is important here to remember how at this time the power or force was understood as a quality *exterior* to the person conducting the rite, even though they had acquired the knowledge or means by which to execute it. This contrasts significantly with modern witchcraft where that power or force is now largely believed to reside *within* the person conducting the rite. Robert Cochrane is a widely known exception to this view.

I must re-iterate here that in all circumstances was it understood, that the gods alone generated the requisite flow of force. The rites were performed sympathetically for the god to mirror, imbuing the rite with reflected virtue. This was the ultimate in theatrical communication, which evolved many hundreds of years later into the sympathetic rites and sacred dramas of Hermetic, micro/macrocosmic events. Of course, an exorcist then, fulfilled the equivalent role of a modern day psychotherapist and worked alongside the physician in the ancient world to restore equilibrium and the metaphysical balance of their patients, aligned in purpose. Modern holistic therapies are heir to this primitive but highly effective practise.

The best magic was invariably prophylactic: each person strived to be moral, honest and charitable. This pleased the gods who would therefore be better disposed to award protection when petitioned or to judge your case favourably when requested. Invocations and prayers were both apotropaic (power to ward off negative forces through use of amulets) and prophylactic (implementation of preventative causalities: the means to administer defence i.e. -medicines/vaccines). Cult images or icons preserved the essence of the gods in order to receive offerings and prayers - again, identity was made through analogy and metaphor. Household shrines once common throughout the ancient world are once again popular, revealing a consistent need for *true* religion within acts of magic. Then as now offerings/libations were given daily to honour and propitiate their deific representatives and mediators.

It is fair to deduce from this understanding of the archaic world a concept of witchcraft as being derived from the Assyrian, Akkadian and Sumerian belief in the power of men and women to perform *sorcerous* acts. Cogently, we may also note that until the end of the 14th century, the English word Wicca (witch), meant specifically a sorcerer. Only later did it evolve into the *heretical* term of a diabolist, where the emphasis rested upon the worship of the Devil and the practise of his black arts. By the Middle Ages, any scholar with access to occult material could perform acts of magic entirely divorced from their original religious contexts; magical acts which had previously been limited only to the priests. Morally and ethically adrift, this dangerous development cross-pollinated with the more generic practises of witchcraft and heretical occultisms, creating a powerful and startling synthesis.

Typically, witches and pagans are illustrated as dancing or moving in circles. Traditionally of course within many religions, circular and serpentine dances were indeed performed *around* either a fire or deific icon! And in folklore, the fairies with whom witches were associated after the 16th century, also danced in rings. Now as then, these are for celebration, prayer and worship and denote sacred space only. They offer no real protective value or purpose except in similar extreme circumstances to those employed in ancient times. A space is charged by <u>intent</u>. The actions are merely theatre for the mind. Remember too, that many temples in the archaic world were formed from the divine and sacred theatres, which were round. History records how many temples did become places of corruption and material production inspiring later Gnostic, Protestant and the now revivalist Wiccan view that:

"where several people commune in my name" –
"be free in your rites!"

Similarly, for ourselves, each rite *is* open, spontaneous and free. It is not rehearsed as scripted theatre. Rather, it is engineered specifically for its advocates to experience the unfolding 'Mystery'.

Freedom of movement is granted in and out of the working area - no barrier exists, indicating an acceptance of the power and force of the gods through nature as omnipresent and omniscient…we are simply the lowest resonant manifestation, and cannot be placed 'beyond' its influence. Ergo, in ritual, we announce ourselves to these (forces) qualities; in awareness of them - we prepare ourselves for their presence. We would never even begin to consider summoning our spirit guides and ancestors to join us. Neither do we seek to control them. This is counter-productive nonsense and simply of no interest. Acts of necromancy and sorcery are both activities many modern practitioners shy from, and are increasingly considered the domain of the ego and the province of the ceremonial magician.

Areas used in modern traditional witchcraft can encompass several sites; movement between them is ardently encouraged. These include locations at caves, hilltops, forests, bridges, lakes - whatever is appropriate to the rite being performed, be that divination, spell-casting or communion. Significance once awarded to the four directions, now 'marked' by the solstices and equinoxes, do in fact register the Sun's most northerly and southerly setting points (south in winter; north in summer). In fact it is by these and other seasonal markers the stars may be observed, anchoring the Heavens to the Earth within the compass.

Annual narratives relating legend, myth and folk history, are dramatized still, through which unfold the themes of creation, existence and evolution in synchronicity with the motion of the stars and the seasons. They are *living* myths, in remembrance of our heritage and lineage as created beings and are in accord with ancient tradition, preserving and continuing our role in the evolution of that legacy. Myth preserves the magic of creation, of life and the mystery of death. Magic has been man's greatest tool because it employs the greatest force - that of mans own Will! Combined with gnosis we thus transcend the spirals of existence to achieve our true purpose. This is perhaps the greatest gift of all, though many who sought it have not prevailed. Over time the Craft has been the natural repository of myth, knowledge and magical practice as these things have declined from use within society, either through suppression, ignorance or ambivalence. Sadly, much of it survives in fragmentary form as folklore or superstition. Other more archaic knowledge has been preserved more discernibly within certain branches of the Traditional Craft.

Myth also celebrates cyclical time; against which annual celebrations of recurrence, suspended in the dreamtime of the eternal present, preserve indelibly the relationship between man, his environment, and the Universe. It is important to assert here the distinction between the cycle of the year and that of time itself. The repetitive progression of the seasons through the year simply illustrates an appropriate vehicle by which the genus of a particular myth unfolds. Each tradition may focus upon the shift of constellations pertinent to them personally, but almost all of them will acknowledge some deference to Cain. As Boötes, the 'farmer' Cain rises, fecunds the Earth; the harvest is reaped, Cain dies. But the myth is not the story of the sowing, and harvesting of the grain associated with this or any other agricultural deity; rather it reveals Cain as the original and eternal progenitor, relating in fact the concept of palingenesis where the cosmic cycle of deification, expressed through the old god as the 'Father' dies, and the new god, his son or younger version of himself is reborn. It is one of sacrifice, dispersal and re-union within itself.

These myths are again linked to the celestial and cosmological micro-macrocosmic relationships of the Earth and the Heavens, giving rise to our calendar, both esoterically and exoterically. Against this symbiosis, the unconscious mind utilises specific symbols that alert the conscious mind of its origins and purpose within this eternal cycle of life that removes the fear of death as a finality. History satisfies the conscious mind, myth satisfies the unconscious mind.

Cain: an agricultural myth?

After the rise of Boötes (the 'ploughman') into the hoary, bleak skies of winter, a meteor shower rains profusely across the northern regions, poetically 'seeding' the hungry Earth, ripe for the first ploughing. Emanating from the region known as the *'Quadrans Muralis'* it may be located on some 19th century star maps (as it was rediscovered in 1835). It occurs near the meeting point of Hercules, Boötes and Draco and is named the Quadrantids after this now obsolete constellation. Up to 101 meteors each hour fall between December 28 and January 7th, peaking around January 3rd-4th and have done so for over 4000 years. The myths suggested in connection with this sacred act of 'creation' are reflected across countless eras and diverse cultures within Europe and beyond. These include the plethora of myths which concern castrated fertility deities from Khronos to Attis, offering a tempting option for associate myths relating the 'lost' phallus' aspect. Osiris is one such figure, also linked intrinsically to agriculture and a distinct 'green' deity.

Myths are rarely to be taken literally; we must peel away the husk to reveal the kernel of wisdom within. The word is veiled and must be charmed from its refuge; paradise after all is a place of hidden wonders, bathed in eternal and effulgent light. Such a garden once graced the pages of many sacred books. So many clues allude to its prominence. Common among these are references to the mystic fire of heaven and of divine grace, but significantly too of life, fertility, and a 'gardener' to oversee it all. Most conspicuous of all is the universal reference to 'The Tree of Life and Knowledge' upon the garden Earth, not a transcendent heaven – it is of the Earth! And so the Truth is really deceptively simple.

To fully appreciate this illuminating narrative, we need to look skyward, as did our ancestors, to follow a pattern easily recognisable with the naked eye and one that encapsulates the cultural myth their belief hinges upon. The star cluster fulfilling this role is focussed upon 'The Plough', around which much folklore asserts some significance within our Northern hemisphere. But here the real focus is the ploughman, who discreetly accompanies 'The Plough' – hidden in plain sight like all true mysteries. Rising in the skies above, this heavenly pedagogue, is there for all with eyes to see. His tale is woven over the ensuing seasons as he moves across the skies and descends briefly before rising again - a perpetual reminder of the cycle of things; of life within eternity. But the seasons are merely a temporal cycle of life upon which is reflected the greater eternal cycle of the cosmos, of the stars and the heavens of both our ancestors and our descendants.

Thus, the ritual year unfolds, a panoply of reflected gnosis:

The Star Compass:

Yule – Cain again begins to rise, slowly, N-NNE.

Reflected in ritual by the rebirth of the Sun/son of light, of life and renewal of life. The Old Horned King, announcing the primal Khaos – light as all potential, shining from within the darkness. Latent Causality.

Twelfth Night – Cain is risen! Arms extending outwards pushing 'The Plough'.

Reflected in ritual as the celebration of the power of the 'Father' perpetuated in the cycle of the Sun/son and the creation of mankind by the generative potential of a living sentient God-force within the universe. Curiously, a shower of meteors – the Quadrantids (of four points) coincidently the most prolific and abundant, burst forth from the east, the region of the rising Cain, seeding the universe with light and power, the semen of the God, for the ritual 'ploughing' of the Earth into the receptive body of the Great Ma. Kinetic causality.

Candlemas – Cain, now a fully risen arc emblazoned across the sky.
See: Star, Hammer & Sickle Glyph.

Reflected in ritual as the expansion and fusion of light and return to Earth of the emerging powers of nature, growth and revealed potential. Manifest causality.

Spring Equinox - Cain approaches close to optimum Zenith.

Reflected in the apogee of the 'Hieros Gamos,' the epic tale of Creation, of 'Zep Tepi', the First Time when man knew the Gods. Harmony, the axial still point. Equilibrium – Zero causality

May's Eve – Cain reaches the Azimuth. He is at his strongest.

Reflected in the verdant virility of the Green Man. Wielding his sickle he becomes both warrior and farmer, generating life, yet holding the potential of death. The male essence, the spirit of the god without. Flux. All causality.

Midsummer – Cain begins his descent, dropping into the western half of the ecliptic.

Reflected in ritual as the sun/son moving into the aspect of the Father becomes once again dormant. Latent causality.

Lammas-tide – Cain's sickle reaches out once again, but upwards, culling the viperous serpent, Draco, reaping the draught of wisdom, she imparts through him.

Reflected in ritual through the Triune Genetrix – the Muse, Fate, Time. Decay. All Being. Manifest causality.

Autumn Equinox – Only half of Cain remains visible above

the ecliptic, but the Council of seven elders, of the Corona Borealis remain in clear view.

Reflected in ritual within variant descent myths and mysteries: ie. the Descent of Inanna who follows her lover, Dumuzzi – 'the farmer and the shepherd – the duality of priest and king' to learn of the cycle of life and death, instigated and witnessed by the Council of Seven. Poise. Equilibrium. Zero causality.

All Hallows – Cain almost sunk on the ecliptic, only his head can be seen. He effectively 'dies' Reflected in ritual by the dismembered skull/severed head and sickle.

Oracular activity and prophetic potencies. Fate. Flux. All causality.

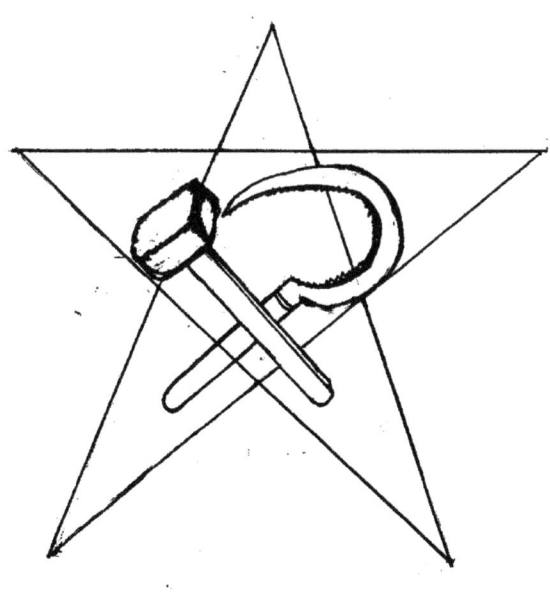

Star, Hammer & Sickle Glyph

As if to illustrate this union of smith-craft and agriculture, the two civilising forces of creative and expansive power that motivate evolution, a gift to mankind, one unique symbol remains outstanding in its simplicity and succinct deference to this principle – that of the soviet star. This curious design, the red pentagram shield (star of Venus), upon which the hammer of Tubal and the sickle of Cain combine. Russia of course was the greatest example of how the union of these forces typify the use and re-use of symbols and glyphs to generate new meaning driven by instinctive recognition of deeper truths. How easily we overlook the obvious. This is the true meaning of occult. To 'see,' we already have to know.

Cain, Kinship, the Egregore and the Triune God

"As ceremony is the soul of the people; and relationships are the heart of the people; so leadership is the mind of the people."[168]

This chapter deals with the structure of the Clan, its politics, foundations and beliefs, specifically by analogous anthropology and known fundamental attributes, both past and present that have nourished the Egregore, the heart and soul of the Clan.

A Supernal Trinity comes from the idea of the *'Trimurti'* known as Brahma, Vishnu and Shiva and within the Hindu sects and practices there will always be conflicting inconsistencies and apparent contradictions. All carry qualities that allude to different aspects within the variant streams of Cainite gnosis within the greater Luciferian corpus. Yet because these aspects are not polarized, as is more typical of Western deific forms, both Shiva and Vishnu specifically possess coterminous merit relative to Lucifer, Cain and even Tubal Cain. Brahma as the remote and nebulous 'All Father' deserves a study dedicated to his mysteries alone, as a cosmic force. He is surely the Old Horn God/King residing in the north representing a more remote Cainite form.

So when comparing Shiva or Vishnu analogously to other forms or potencies, we should specify what particular aspects we are alluding to, in order to avoid confusion. As for archaic deific forms, because Vishnu has become manifest through various notable avatars, we have linked him to the more Promethean form of the arcane Enki, rather than Enlil, for whom a parallel may be discerned within the remote ascetic, Shiva. With regard to the dynamic between Vishnu (Abel) and Shiva (Cain), a shift in perspective is requisite. Shiva the destroyer is considered to be the 'hunter' having lunar correspondents, whereas Vishnu as preserver is the solar farmer; but because other qualities overlay these perspectives, the matter becomes more complex.

Shiva is the recluse, the ascetic, and orthodoxy denies him incarnations, Vishnu has several, including Krishna, all of whom have dedicated themselves to assisting mankind to evolve, through Khaos if need be. Both Shiva and Vishnu have dedicants, devotees and worshippers, either through *gnani* or bhakti (respectively). One is intellectual and austere, the other is emotional and of the heart; both transpose to Apollo and Dionysus very well. Following that through it is actually Shiva, who like Cain could best be described as wild and shamanic, albeit not strictly so. Similarly, Abel may be compared favourably to Vishnu having no fixed presence upon the Earth, for he is Lord of the celestial regions. In fact, placed upon the 'tree' we discover where they are best suited: Chesed (*Vishnu*) and Geburah (*Shiva*), and a better graft than Binah and Chockmah who are higher placed than these Tanist deities.

Aspected in ancient times as 'winds,' Varuna, Agni and Indra are the titanic forms of Brahma, Shiva and Vishnu, which gives us some idea of their elemental qualities and potencies. Varuna is 'The universal encompasser, the all-embracer, maker and upholder of Heaven and Earth.' He was the monarch of all things, be they man or God, beast or planet, knowledge and gifts of nature. He is even associated by some with Mitra, ruling night and day between them. His position devolved with the rise of the new gods, the '*Adityas*'²²⁸ eventually acquiring the qualities of Poseidon, symbolized by the fish (Odel Rune - archaic wind of the waters?), though he is not specially connected with actual bodies of water in the form of seas or rivers, but more of the atmosphere.¹⁷⁰

Indra, god of the firmament, embodies the manifest atmosphere. He is associated with Vayu, as the wind god. His weapons are those by which he ensnares his 'foe' (the unrelenting and searing drought): the thunderbolt, arrows, a hook, and a net, which he also uses to generate rain, lightning and thunder. The Romans equated him with Jupiter (*Chesed*) and his domain was air.¹⁷¹ Agni has three forms of manifestation: in the celestial regions as the Sun, in the air as lightning and upon the Earth (his particular dominion) as natural fire. Together this triad of gods ruled over the Earth, air and sky. Agni mediates between men and the gods, bears witness to their actions and protects them from harm.

Of all, fire is the most sacred element. Agni is represented with seven flaming tongues, each having a distinct name cognate with the remaining seven guardians of the compass. Known as Lokapalas²³¹ each of these eight deities/winds are accompanied by their requisite spousal Shakti and totemic beast or vehicles of ascent and descent (totalling again the enigmatic '24') preside over the four cardinal and four intermediate points of the compass as follows and are again reflected within the runes. The Hindu compass places these winds as follows:

(1.) Indra, east; (2.) Agni, southeast; (3.) Yama, south; (4.) Surya, southwest; (5.) Varuna, west; (6.) Vayu, northwest; (7.) Kuvera, north; (8.) Soma, northeast.¹⁷³

So again we witness a seven plus one system derived from the three within which we have, after the 'Father,' divine twins of complementary yet paradoxically, opposing forces, known as 'Tanist'. There is of course an alternative legend where, rather than Enki and Eve being the parents of Cain, we have Adam and Lilith as the parents of Cain, though not of Abel in either case. With regard to the Tanist element within various cosmologies be they Gnostic, Pagan or Hebraic, the following statement brings to bear certain parallels of particular importance between them:

> "Similarly, some Jewish Gnostic myths have Cain born of Eve without copulation with Adam, sometimes as a result of congress with the serpent. The implication is that Samael Yaldaboath, the demiurge, had intercourse with Eve and conceived Cain. However, the texts themselves are not clear on this point. Cain and Abel have female companions in Sophia and Eve.
>
> In the Babylonian star lore, the archaic 'Agrarian Worker' implies farming, but really means pastoral, which is explicitly livestock over grain. The first domesticated farm animal was sheep, hence shepherds. Abel, as we know, was a shepherd. Interestingly, within the images and description of the Clan Stang by E. John Jones' writing, he makes particular mention of a ram positioned at the head. Opposing this image is the sickle at the foot. This seems to reflect the lower and upper selves in the Stang represented by the divine twins so very common throughout mythology, exampled in: Gilgamesh and Enkidu, Romulus and Remus, to name but two. The two horns atop the Stang might suggest the twins, particularly relative to the twin pillars. Therefore, it is a grave mistake to dismiss Abel in preference to Cain, as one is simply an aspect of the other, indeed a defining characteristic that composes the other. The harmony of such pairings could be suggested in the third - Eros, Seth, the divine child?"[174]

Indeed this insightful motif is employed to great effect in ancient narrative where one aspect of deity takes precedence over another and is deemed to assume his Virtue. Marduk and Ninurta were two such figures noted as usurping Enki and Enlil respectively. Further more, this insightful exploration of the myths of Cain and Abel, the view of the Fall, of Cain and the angelic/Watchers further exemplifies that the actual mythos within the Clan of Tubal Cain shares but few principles common to many others within the Luciferian spectrum of belief and practise. Naturally we do view them as Tanist (composed of protagonist and antagonist), each a vital counterpart to the other and one incarnate/mortal and one discarnate/immortal (best exemplified in the Greek twins Castor and Pollux) and whose correlation with the farmer and shepherd reflect many of these archaic myths of rival 'twins' who present and retain this dynamic. Thus Cain the farmer is represented by the sickle and Abel the pastoral shepherd by the ram.

Cain 'overcame' his brother, where semantics is everything. Cain is of divine (immortal) 'blood' (read avatar of spirit), Abel is the son of Adam, doomed to 'die.' Seth represents the race of man, also born of Adam, whose soul is 'human'. We have the spirit of Cain or Abel within us, the seeker or the sleeper, the wanderer/hermit/mendicant or the person of roots, of material distraction, of worldly concerns. We do not perceive Cain as the negative 'first murderer.' Rather, for us he is the evolutionary catalyst, the anarchic principle of challenge and change, of innovation etc, who dared to stimulate the 'status quo.' The nomadic god of shepherdic *Hapiru* (Hebrews), Yahweh, storm god (Enlil) was presented by his followers as being unaccepting of these changes (resistance to change) and subsequently 'cast him out'. This rejection by his tribe, was, and still is a typical reaction to any challenge to prescribed tradition.

Effectively exiled and forced to be that which he'd despised, his curse for wishing to introduce change among his tribal people was to become a nomad, an eternal wanderer, never at peace, and never to settle.

His 'mark' (we believe) is that by which he was known or recognized by - his city-building and civilizing gnosis, advancing and evolving societies encountered by him as he wandered across the globe. The 'mark' of the anarchic innovator is always in the work undertaken and achieved, the changes made by them (ie. he left his 'mark'). We do not believe it to be a physical mark in the form of a brand, tattoo or deformity. It is unlikely though not impossible that it could be a 'spiritual' mark because this would already have had to be present at birth and would have been the driving force of his atavistic dynamism. The mark could also have had an additional presence in the form of a building tool such as the square, or compass, a chisel, hammer et cetera and can also be translated as 'sign.' This could of course mean almost anything including a magical seal/sigil, perhaps a password or handshake, introducing yet more speculative elements and associations.

Again this is merely one view presented within the Clan's distinctive mythos and remains considerably different to others within the Craft in general. Other concepts similarly diverge, yet which retain the integrity of earlier faiths and beliefs absorbed by the cumulative and continuously evolving Egregore of the Clan. These idiosyncratic beliefs and developments must nonetheless be set within the greater context of 'Clanship' in order to realize the bonded significance of such an archaic social unit. Insight will then encourage a more visionary perception of how a Clanship operates, especially with regard to the three sets of mysteries (male, female and priestly) of the Clan of Tubal Cain specifically. So it has become essential at this point to explore the development and significance of the 'Clanship' across Northern Europe, including England ('Ing'land).

Historically three classes existed within Germanic society, not indistinct to the tripartite caste system of India and the Clanships of Scandinavia. Each maintained a 'provider' level, composed of farmers or manual labourers; above them a warrior class existed to protect and defend. Governorship of a Clan was executed through an elite or noble class of priests, teachers, kings and law-makers. In particular, the Scandinavian Clan or '*ætt*' as one such social group expresses the practise of belonging based on common descent or on the formal acceptance/adoption into the group at a '*þing*' (thing).[175]

A Clan then is a very specific term which determines a group of people united by actual or perceived kinship and descent. Clan members will frequently recognize a founding member or apical ancestor where actual lineage patterns remain improvable or unknown. Kinship-based bonds may also be only symbolical in nature, where all people within the Clan share this 'given' (common) ancestor that symbolizes their identity and cohesion as a 'family.' This ancestor is however, not always human and will then be referred to as an atavistic totem. Clans are generally described as kin-ship based tribes or sub-groups of tribes such as bands, despite cultural differences, especially where the distinguishing factor is that a Clan is often a smaller part of a larger society such as a tribe, a chiefdom, or a state. Typically this applies to Clans of Scottish, and Irish provenance where Clan is a derivative of 'clann' signifying offspring or descendants (ie. 'children').

A noteworthy exception to this family construct is the Norse *ätter*[176] which cannot be translated to refer to a tribe or band; a more accurate translation is to a 'house' or 'lineage.' These dynastic preferences were not bound into birthright, but by election or force of arm. This is because, within the Celtic language group of peoples, physical 'blood' groups define a Clan, whereas for Germanic and Norse peoples, adoption into a Clan was possible by marriage or special favour; it was often a matter of following a particular aspect of deity through whom the named ancestor would claim descent bound in an oath-bound allegiance. The eponymous personage to whom any Clan becomes known by is generally derived from just such a primal ancestor. There was no individual ownership of land property or estate, rather the leader of each 'house' or Clan governed a prescribed section of his people and kins-folk.

> "In summary, therefore, after the end of the "core" dynastic period in each Anglo-Saxon kingdom, it is probably safer to assume that each small family group of succeeding monarchs was unrelated to its predecessors, unless corroborative evidence exists in primary sources which support the existence of such relationships. In the following document, care has been taken to highlight where reported descents are dubious."[177]

Some other Clans are bilateral, consisting of all the descendants of the apical ancestor through both the male and female lines of which the Irish and Scottish Clans are examples. Jewish peoples are generally defined mainly as the Clan of descendants from *one* male ancestor in blood (Jacob) and *four* female ancestors (Leah, Rachel, Bilhah and Zilpah). These examples of patrilineal, matrilineal, or bilateral Clanships are dependent upon the kinship rules and mores of each distinct societal ethnicity.

> "A main element uniting Germanic societies is kingship, in origin a sacral institution combining the functions of military leader, high priest, law-maker and judge. Germanic monarchy was elective, the king was elected by the free men from among eligible candidates of a family tracing their ancestry to the tribe's divine or semi-divine founder.
>
> In early Germanic society, the free men of property each ruled

their own estate and were subject to the king directly, without any intermediate hierarchy as in later feudalism. Free men without landed property could swear fealty to a man of property who as their lord would then be responsible for their upkeep, including generous feasts and gifts. This system of sworn retainers was central to early Germanic society, and the loyalty of the retainer to his lord was taken to replace his family ties."[178]

Germanic peoples congregated in natural woodland groves, under *'Gardh'* trees not dissimilar to their fellow 'Celts' though rarely, if ever, did they concede to artificial temple constructions. Offerings, given as Blót or Sumble form the genus of worship practiced by the ancient Germanic and Scandinavian people, resembling cognate practises of the Celts and Balts. Occasionally a pile of rough stones known as a *'horgr'*[179] acted as a rude altar. Yet the priestly class of the Germanic peoples never achieved the professional and semi-hereditary kudos or form enjoyed by the Druidic class within Celtic society. It has been speculated that because magical and shamanic traditions were essentially the preserve of woman, known as *'Völvas,'* Germanic kingship developed tangentially to that within 'Celtic society,' accelerating the sacral role of priest to priest-king. The priest or *'gothi,'* as the head of a kindred group of families was responsible for the welfare of his people and his duty required his administration of all necessary sacrifice for his people.

A primal being, named Heimdall guards the Rainbow Bridge (Bifrost) arching upwards to the realm of the Gods in Asgard. Each one of the Nine Worlds drafted upon and around Irminsul/Yggdrasil has mythical significance to specific events that have or will occur. Foremost of these is Valhalla, the grave hall of the slain, of Odhin, placed within Asgard, where the most heroic warriors (*Einherjar*) selected specifically by the

Valkyries reside until summoned once again to defend the gods during Ragnarok.

These Nine Worlds are generally expressed as the following:[180]

- **Asgard**, world of the Aesir (Eastern plane).

- **Vanaheimr**, world of the Vanir.

- **Midgard,** world of humans (Middle plane).

- **Muspellheim**, world of the primordial element of fire (Blacksmiths (Muorsh Eiron) home).

- **Niflheim**, world of the primordial element of ice.

- **Svartálheim**, world of the Svartálfar (black elves) (possibly Surt).

- **Alfheimr**, world of the Álfar (elves).

- **Hel**, underground world of the dead. Oath-breakers and other nefarious law-breakers are said to suffer torturous ordeals for their crimes in Niflhel, a sub realm of Hel.

- **Jötunheimr**, world of the Jötnar (Giants).

Rich mythologies from both sources relate tales of curious lists or classes of beings known as archaic 'Clans' of animistic nature spirits (Vaettir). Named the Aesir and Vanir, they were later perceived or expressed as the 'Old Gods'; to them we may add the Jötnar, the Álfar and Dvergar. Beyond this, we may include the realm of spirits or the dead who reside within the shadowy Underworld. The Aesir and Vanir Clans, though once warring factions in pre-history long ago organized a truce, thereafter reigning collectively as the Aesir.[181]

Yet other strange beasts populate this mythical landscape including three described as the progeny of Loki: the fearsome Fenris, a monstrous wolf, who is of prime significance in Ragnarok; Jörmungandr the titanic sea-serpent (or 'worm') that coils around Midgard; and last but by no means least is Hel, ruler of Helheim. After Odhin sacrificed his eye in Mimir's Well during his quest for wisdom, the two companions of Odhin, the ravens Huginn and Munnin (thought and memory, respectively) became his watchers who kept him abreast of the affairs of man within Midgard. Most famous of all is Loki's son, the eight legged 'stead' that transported Odhin between and throughout the nine realms.

Now we have established the basic structure of deity and cosmological landscape, intimated the shades of the ancestors, it now behoves us to move onto the concepts of Suzerainty within the Clan of Tubal Cain which is quite different from Sovereignty, yet ironically, both are to a great extent founded upon gender. The word gender comes from the Latin 'genus' meaning 'kind', 'type', or 'sort'. This is tentatively sourced from a root gen- giving us kin, kind, king, among others. The use of 'gender' in reference to masculinity and femininity as 'types,' is commonly attested, particularly since the 14th century.

Gender, relates to the spectrum of characteristics and attributes that are perceived to distinguish between 'males' and 'females,' extending from one's biological sex to one's social role (gender identity). In general parlance, it is used interchangeably with 'sex' to denote the condition of being male or female. But the theory that human nature is essentially epicene, where social distinctions based on sex are arbitrarily constructed is quite significant. All matters regarding this theoretical process of social construction have been labelled as matters of gender. So is gender attribution biological, social or cultural?

As a tradition entrenched heavily within an archaic and quite specific mythos, we do fulfil gender based roles that are formed as socially imposed constructs albeit imposed through the analogical parameters of our mythos; but even so, because of the immense geographical and aeonic expanse of its fundamental tenets, these transcend all cultural constraints. Biology is undeniably a factor in this. Nevertheless, categorizing males and females into specific social roles creates binaries/polarities, in which individuals feel they have to be at one end of an artificially imposed linear spectrum and must identify themselves (unnaturally) as a man or woman. These artificial 'boundaries' have generated much political debate, spawning a great many theories regarding why and how gender is applied.

Saturn, rules all boundaries yet his impositions urge us to exceed them, to transcend and evolve our understanding. To achieve this we must first explore and assimilate all that exists within those boundaries before turning our attention to those without. Conventional roles ascribed to mythological concepts facilitate this, actuating by accumulation the epicene nature of our genus. All mystical and especially Gnostic traditions have utilized this pedagogical methodology to great effect through individual anagogical epiphanies. In many mystical traditions, especially of the Kabbalah, the Shekinah represents the feminine aspect of God's essence. Christianity considers the Holy Spirit as neuter.

Returning again to the Hindu model, 'male' gods are vitalized by 'female' virtue via their '*Shakti*s.' Only through unification of both does Shiva become the Cosmic Lord. In the absence of Shakti, he is deemed lifeless, and fails to achieve his potential. Hinduism expresses that each human carries within himself both male and female elements that are *forces* rather than *sexes*, the union of which through realization brings Truth. This understanding obliterates all material distinction between male and female completely. Within the Clan of Tubal Cain, we follow this archaic assignation of Virtue, which is perceived as neutral, to manifest within the corporeal female, the lesser form of the Moon in order that she fulfils this role in reflection of the greater cosmic myth both she and the Magister of the Clan embody.

To deny or attempt to alter this balanced pattern would negate the whole mythos upon which it is predicated. Of course in theory a Magister could hold Virtue for the Clan and a Maid could uphold the Law/Covenant, but such a reversal would serve no good purpose. Their mysteries are taught separately at first only to give definition to the third set of mysteries by which they are transcended. Only through initial and primary study of these biased roles does this third neuter role become vividly experienced. These roles are gender biased, and deliberately so - but so finely tuned are the Clan's rituals, they facilitate the requisite Gnostic apprehension of the numinous devoid of all but their own truths. Other traditions will find other ways to fulfil these criteria.

Ours is totally distinct from modern paganisms and the diverse and idiosyncratic variations of Wicca, where the emphasis on Goddess worshipping facilitates the assumption by the woman as 'High Priestess' taking precedence, adopting a superior role distinctly absent from most Traditional Craft practises wherein the Magister 'heads' or leads the Clan. In Wicca, the High Priestess chooses her High Priest and together they perpetuate a disparate and somewhat awkward mythos based entirely on their *sexual* rather than *gender* roles. In the Clan of Tubal Cain, the Magister mediates for his stream through his chosen Maid who holds it.

This is an important distinction; the Maid receives Virtue in order for her to actuate her gender role within the mysteries, distinct of her sex. This ensures that with her as his filter, the egregoric Virtue remains balanced. He appoints her (unlike Wicca) and, if the stream acknowledges that choice, she may claim Virtue from him. This delegation is not a product consigned to their era and to Robert Cochrane and to E.J. Jones but to countless mystical traditions as mentioned earlier. Wicca asserts an imbalance through its negation of the male and male deific status. Believing that gnosis occurs only where a balanced understanding exists, all notion of deific preference is rejected within the Clan. Our mysteries reflect and generate this process of evolution.

Naturally, when a Magister is without a Maid, he retains Virtue, but as an unbalanced force, not because he is 'male' but because he is unable to express the mysteries by himself within a Clan context. This does not negate his personal ability to access and fulfil his own evolution through neuter spirit as an individual. But for those within his Clan, for whom he represents and embodies its tutelary deity, he manifests what is mediated. He thus becomes the '*Lord of this World*' and she the heavenly or otherworld noumena. These roles cannot be reversed through our male and female sex based units, although they are experienced via their dedicated gender based mysteries.

When Robert Cochrane abused his 'role,' he forfeited his *right* and ability to manifest her Shakti based Virtue, (as in the mythological barren kings) and thus relinquished it to E. J. Jones. After his death, his widow then relinquished her 'hold' on the Virtue also. Both were effectively returned to the source, the egregore of the Clan; some, though by no means all Traditional groups uphold this archaic formulae of Covenanted, feudal and archaic Suzerainty.

Those most likely to follow a more androcentric locus are predictably the ones based in the late 18th century crafts and guilds of horsemen, traditions of cunning-men, pellars and such forth. Generally speaking (and again there are exceptions) these tend not to have such mystical aspirations as those which follow the more archaic traditions of the Luciferian stream. Robert Cochrane was torn between the two. On the one hand his family upheld the code of the horsemen and pellars, but this became superannuated when he received a more 'inspired' mediation from a more archaic place. With John's help and substantial input, he was able to formulate a vibrant 'tradition' fuelled by a primal force, yet accessible through a conventional compass, effectively anchoring the mysteries within it.

Suzerainty is often considered to be a concept of political superiority that depicts a structural condition that may imply Sovereignty, though not necessarily. As such it could as easily depict a simple state of control and authority invested into an elected office. Sovereignty has been expressed as an authority that held its foundation in the mediation of God's Will, or in other words to be in accordance with the Divine Order of the People and its sovereign territories. Within certain ancient cultures we know that a divine state of Sovereign communion with the Divine Order or God is achieved by being in a state of concord with the Fertile Lands as the King and the Land are seen to be ONE.

Modern dictionaries present a meaning of it perceived through any given current political climate, but in fact more traditionally, Suzerainty is applied to feudalism, and all the principles of vassalage, liege lords etc. What this means effectively, is that a Lord (primarily, and his Lady) hold sway via an oath over his/her people, with all parties duty bound under its sacrosanct mutually obligatory premise declared in troth to the god/s of those people. This implies therefore a divine authority too. More importantly its distinction from sovereignty rests in the sacred and indivisible bond between its people with each other and with its leader - hence 'Clanship.' Conversely sovereignty refers to a land based rule and/or authority in which people may live, occupy or exist upon freely without obligation to or from its sovereign. Nomadic or migrating peoples such as gypsies for example, no matter where they are remain a collective people, unbound by the sovereign whose country they inhabit.

During the feudal Middle Ages anyone not privileged or titled was required to offer fealty to their liege lord (rather than the King/Queen) in exchange for protection and spiritual leadership. Simply put - the monarch, having dominion based on territory ruled the land, but lords and ladies, had dominion through oath of its people (no matter where or in what country they were). Vikings and 'Celts' especially adhered to this premise with countless fiefdoms, who were invariably called upon to become mercenaries for the sovereign monarch. As all Clans in that era believed a descent to a tutelary deity, divine kingship was not exclusive, and moreover, kingship was invariably challenged and won by right of arm. As the Clan of Tubal Cain are and remain a 'people' aligned to a perceived tutelary deity (real or mythical) we are subject to the principle of suzerainty. Wherever we are, the Suzerain is paramount, independently and irrespective of any monarch.

We are *not* however, geocentric, but draw Virtue from an ancestral lineage of people, centred not in the land, therefore no 'blood acre.' Our whole cosmology denies geocentricity. We remain firmly aligned to the histories of its peoples. A 'people' subsumes its gods through evolution and progress, but a geocentric monarchy may not. Any faith rooted in the land is tied to that of its ruling monarch (think of Old Hal), in this way the faith itself is at the mercy of war or conquest. The 'nomad' on the other hand retains the faith of his ancestors - I follow the gods of my 'father's father' etc. Virtue is of the line, then, not land, not even mythically.

In the archaic world, all kings and all leaders were understood as having divine descent; only when overall kingship established supreme rulership of collective territories did the premise of a singular 'divine' Monarchy supported by a land based religious body. This instigated essential dogma to maintain control. This is why *'Gnostics'* have a history of being travelling mendicants - *bound by no land or state*. When they failed to observe this, they became victim to virtual genocide. With regard to more mythical cycles, the welfare of a people was subject to that of its Lord/Duc, NOT necessarily its monarch. This welfare, through the political agendas of the later Middle Ages (after the War of the Roses witnessed the decline of feudalism in fact) became retrospectively re-interpreted to support the concepts of an overall divine kingship, so that it would be beyond question or reproach by peers of the realm, who ironically thereafter became subject 'peers' bound by oath to serve and support the realm (land and sovereignty) of its monarch. In this nifty act, the former responsibilities of the lord became the kings and the people became subject to the mercy and welfare of the monarch. This is allegedly one of the charges made against those accused in the witch trials of this period - the failure to acknowledge a sovereign, making it a treasonable offence. The Craft thus became in one sense anarchic through its insistence to adhere to earlier feudalisms.

Of course, monarchs were said to have 'married' the land or the sea for many thousands of years, but this again became the locus of land grabs by power mongers who in taking the queen, owned the land she represented. Helen of Sparta was one such queen. Her story is rarely given truthfully as a principle where Menelaus had to retrieve her to prevent Paris from claiming Sparta! Arthur too had the same problem with Gweneffyr. Legends and sagas reveal the history of conquest; myth reveals the lament of its spirituality lost in those struggles. These evolve and change through the eras and peoples who relate them. Nevertheless, these remain the tales that formulate the racial and political agendas of coalescing cultural identities. Locked within such tales are kernels of Truth that become lost to the greater narrative. In the Fisher King[182] article the challenge was laid to accepted opinion that had determined the king required the return of the 'feminine' Grail/power/virtue to become healed and fit again to rule and heal his land. This is of course only partially true (as above). In fact the Grail is only 'feminine' in its complementary quality genitivally associated with - ie: wisdom.

The king has lost his way, his faith and as the priest/king his people are bereft - the barren landscape in which they starve is a graphic only, a narrative device, a literary motif of the mystical writers. His faith/wisdom (Pistis-Sophia) needs restoration and re-union within the *Hieros Gamos* to restore his Virtue. The Grail has nothing to do with the land or womanhood in the absolute sense. This association was made by linking Pistis Sophia with Mary in the Marionanism of that period in order to again promote the role of the Church in the blessed rightness and ability of its chosen monarch to rule.

Again, the idea of male gods and heroes sacrificed to themselves is a later Christian gloss on the early myths of immolation and self-mutilation that formed the journey of many ancient religions, revealing more about their primitive brutality than their spirituality. More enlightened descent myths of a Promethean nature do of course reveal an element of 'punishment' by the older gods for bringing wisdom to mankind, a punishment they willingly accept, but this is not the same as willingly sacrificing oneself for their own knowledge as did Odhin, an act that also had nothing to do with maidens, altruism, or salvation of humanity.

Many kings actively engaged in near annihilation of all family contenders who might usurp them. Queens were political acquisitions whose 'blood-line' was unimportant. Their dowered lands, however, were. Because the Grail is gnosis/wisdom, anyone may therefore be a seeker - the Grail is pure and may be won by the true pilgrim; that is all that we believe; no more no less. It has nothing to do with monarchs, land, fertility, just the pursuit of Truth.

The mythos of a people is its people and while the egregore must evolve through growth of awareness and the mediating perceptions of an ever increasing spiritual alignment, change must become a natural development of that unconsciously. Conscious change is rooted in subjectivity, human frailty, desire etc and therefore manipulated against the Truth to which the egregore must remain bound. As individuals, the links are forged through the cumulative experiences of ancestral souls through whom the mythos has served as a vehicle for their evolution within the mysteries. We may change form, style, praxes etc, but not the core - which is the egregore itself! We may change our perceptions and our approach, how we teach etc, but the Luciferian premise, the Gnostic principalities of the Clan must remain. It is this Truth that shines as a beacon, it is what people recognize, it is what they feel when introduced to it; it is a true tradition. We do not deny either sex the Grail, nor do we deny either sex their experience of the divine. Our methods and teachings are structured, but each person is treated as an individual and their journey is engineered specifically for them within the mythos.

Science has verified gender oriented functions of the left and right brain, not in opposition, but complementary, but they do present themselves distinctly and for ease of terminology, understanding and application are aligned to gender. As highlighted earlier we must all transcend these, ultimately. It is felt that the myths do in themselves need alternative presentation, possibly even re-interpretation, and so attempts here are made to remove the many glosses that have built up from those exoteric writers on the outside of their truths, in order to allow the new seekers a journey free of political and religious dogma and obfuscation.

Hindu chauvinism along with the Grail mysteries of the medieval era do in fact typify the spiritual evolution for men on the back of women; but the fact that human error/ego/bias has failed a glorious and sublime principle, should not prevent us from utilising it to its full and desired fruition. The harmony is here one of equality, a union of *force and form*. It is not about supremacy or subjugation nor a lack of one for the other. Within Gnosticism this imbalance was not engaged or indulged; both men and women as individuals achieved enlightenment supported by their community. It is essential that even within partnerships the journey is an individual one partnered through evolution of spirit only, not a manifest spouse, but each person must know him/herself fully in mind, soul and spirit to accomplish this; we cannot deny our nature, just transcend it, we cannot reject our sex, just assimilate it; this is true sacrifice, the full realization of what we are in order to become something else.

The titanic primalities are qualities than generate evolution by their very chaos and flux, the tempering of these by order is the sentience of mankind prior to the 'fall', that is his loss of that primal innocence. By this no moral sense is implied, but simply a sense of things, of separation from the source as the ego developed exponentially into Will. Any woman may learn the principles of sacrifice in order to evolve, though we do not need to associate ourselves with self-immolation through a male hero motivated by themes of self-glorification and immortality on the manifest plane, the true message of Christ is not to be found on the tree. The titanic, primal forces are of creation rather than of nature, which distinguishes them from fertility and from the land; they are in fact cosmological. We consider the celestial causalities as primary, not land, we seek harmony with the source, not Gaia.

Within the Clan of Tubal Cain this instigated the 'fall' as above, our disconnection, our humanity was reflected back onto the primal forces and they became debased and trivial; the divine flame is beyond this and is the essence by which we may aspire to transcend the hyle, the form of our nature. We seek to transcend this form through knowledge not of the deities we created but the forces that created enlightened and now guide us, if we allow them access. Of course things may change but this would reflect a lack of understanding of the purpose in the distinct roles of Maid and Magister, which are not bound in dogma but in the reflection of the Maid as the Tree of Life and the Magister as the Priest King who as supreme psychopomp becomes entombed (like Merlin) within it rather than upon it; not sacrificed, but preserved to speak, through the leaves, its knowledge. We of course have the Covenant, a Law that binds the people to it, a concept of destiny through surrender.

Obviously such metaphors do maintain the concepts of mediation and embodiment within our mythos to gender, yet as afore-mentioned, there is no purpose served for a reversal of roles, nothing is to be gained by women fixating upon the Law, because as Maid she teaches those mysteries that all may transcend them in true gnosis, and similarly for any man to be fixated upon holding Virtue, rather than teaching its qualities for transcendence among the female mysteries, is again to miss their purpose. Ego becomes an uneasy distraction, a manifest obsession. Virtue is surely more nebulous, a link to the Source; a force of identity, a sentience that guides, again not bound by myth or geography?

Our mythos holds no tenets regarding the virgin, fertility aspect in land or womb, hence our mysteries remain unconcerned with such matters, seeking transcendence through gnosis beyond such human diversions. We are, very simply a 'people' under the tutelage of a guiding tribal deity, which gives us a collective identity not anchored in anything but that force. A tribal or tutelary deity is Clan/family specific, being named for it. Its beliefs concern only that named Clan and does not relate to any landscape, be it literal or one borne of myth.

Nomadic peoples have never considered themselves linked to the land. And within any Clan, again all family members do pledge allegiance to each other and their tutelary deity. This has created the egregore we now serve. There are many streams leading to the ocean, and we are none of us the ocean. Though the ocean is our common goal, the geography we all navigate may differ, and the tools required to circumvent obstacles may therefore be different and this is not a problem and devalues no one's route. Our perspective is not in any way literal. The work is immensely experiential, very fluid, exceptionally diverse and absolutely seeker specific. They are each encouraged to discover for themselves an understanding that keys them into the spirit of the egregore. We cannot provide it and we cannot teach it. We cannot presume to know their Fate.

We also absolutely support all seekers to attain. In this each individual is guided by signs and portents given by spirit in circumstances irrelevant of gender. The seeker is a seeker and the Grail is gnosis. All myth is valuable and the more so because we use it objectively, remaining unanchored to any myth cycle/system. We pursue Truth, and have forged a way that works for us. Others do it differently. This is good. Within the Clan of Tubal Cain, historical facts are used as a platform upon which myth has been explored to shift our awareness of both, linking mythical progenitors and historical ancestors within a gnosis based egregore, effectively as an intimate introduction beyond the current context and incarnation of the Clan as an extant group. We are a 'people,' not of a book, not of a land, but of a particular ancestry. Our history is complex, our spirituality is not.

History and myth combine to weave a pattern that determines a group identity. Our tutelary deity is one assigned to its ancestral people. Our spirit is a collective that has evolved from this origin. We like many others, traverse a mythic landscape and engage in metaphor, but this is of little use to anyone not engaged in our mysteries under the tutelage of that deity. Discussion of these principles is almost impossible, confined sublimely to experience. The options for discussion then are primarily restricted to how we approach that and how we understand the dynamics that have created such experiences. This involves how each tradition functions, which is dependent upon belief structure. Yet if the mysteries do not engage in the history of its adherents then how are its descendents to evolve in Truth? There can be no validation of context if the context cannot be traced laterally, mythically and retrospectively. Triangulation plots the course of Truth.

Where we then express those mysteries is of course the compass and successful navigation of it requires a map that visually plots the Merkavah through its course. In thinking about the 4th and 5th dimensions of time and quantum space, we may say that just as the compass is the vehicle for exploration beyond the eight physical markers around the periphery formed by the cardinal and cross quarter points, these two extra dimensions are suggested and generated by the others, being outside the visible realms. Genuine Kabbalists will accept that the Tree is open to insightful interpretation, and do not profess a dogmatic approach, so no heresy there. Our own work with it could be considered equally heretical by those who are unable to get past rigid correspondences. Although even within the Kabbalah there are different schools where some use the Tiphoretic mediation to ascend, while others draw it down and upon themselves for magical work. Everything is a two way process especially for those who understand how true mediation works.

Similarly with alchemy, as a trans-formative process, it has always generated a fascinating and multifarious application. Some may qualify Yesod as fire, others as air, while we ourselves perceive it as water, the fluid realm of the unconscious, of dreamscapes, illusion and subversive realities. This mutability is precisely so amenable when working with the Kabbalah where the perspective shifts everything accordingly. Where the Kabbalah has its own cosmogony, it is utterly rigid, as it does express through geometry the formation of worlds. According to the Sefer Yetzirah, the Three mothers = fire, air and water (not elemental but cosmic) created the fathers, and from them the progeny; from the mothers, Aleph Mem and Shin manifest body (water), soul (air) and spirit (fire) into men and women (progeny) as divisive products, that is the elements men and women controlled became separated as follows:

men: Air,   Earth   and   *Fire.*
women: Air,   Earth   and   *Water*

Robert Cochrane does discuss the 'Three Mothers' are Aleph, Mem and Shin (air, water and *fire*), in the letters, but they are quite distinct from the three (manifest) *elements* given to *womankind*, being Earth, air and water, where fire is given to man alone. Man is the manifest form of divine fire (all creation and inspiration) and may thus control it. They therefore share air and Earth drawing together fire and water to form the manifest yab/yum for earthly genesis. Each therefore requires the other for completion (not as an issue of gender or sex, but on a purely soul level) man's fire and woman's water generates the sacred hexagram. The three mothers are NOT women, are NOT elements, but primal forces - this is the Triune Creatrix, personified in Kali, Hekate, the three veils etc.

Here again is the importance of the aforementioned Trinity being acknowledged, but it must be remembered that it is only Christian Kabbalists who consider Kether, Chockmah and Binah to represent THE trinity of father, son and holy ghost - others do not, in fact, none of them adhere to this concept - as strictly speaking, the Source is beyond the Tree altogether and yet all is within it. All Sephiroth (including the Supernals) are merely emanations from the Source, aspects that progressively descend, no more, no less - hence they are all 'angelic' principles of Virtue and not 'God' per se. Yet may we perceive the Supernals as part of the Manifest World rather than lying beyond the Veil?

Of course, in a metaphysical sense all should be deemed supernatural; nothing can really be expressed as manifest or unmanifest. Rather they are emanations, or essences of increasing manifestation within our plane of conscious awareness, their qualities simply relay cosmological concepts in relation to each other, and our compass allows us to explore these, as do Kabbalists upon Otz Chim. Moreover, they are not beyond reach for specific rituals, where we reach into and beyond the veil. In fact, the veils are just that, not blockades, but semi-permeable translucencies. Even the negative veils surround the Tree and are not truly separate from it or the Source; all are connected within and to it. And this is precisely where Gnosticism merges with Mysticism.

Patterns of Transformation: the Alchemy of Being

Alchemy: Science of God, a gift from the Watchers to mankind. The nature of metallurgy and/or transmutation of matter into spirit.

"...and Beroalde was bidden to climb this tree if he would gain the fruit. He therefore took of the Spiritual Mercurius and Spiritual Sol from the fountains, and anointing himself was carried high into the tree, where he underwent the seven transmutations. He became a volume, a cloud, a star, a pinnacle, a faun, a song, a dream; he ate the fruit and drank the mixed draught, and was wedded to the Queen Soteris in the mystical marriage. And when he returned to the ground, he carried with him a book containing one leaf, and in it written: 'In the sixth hour of the night, search nothing but thyself and thou shalt find the first matter of the stone, and in no other place in the whole wide world shalt thou find it'..."[183]

Throughout the history of this amazing Craft, many famous men and women including Hermes Trismegistus, Imhotep, Iamblichus, Isis and Miriam/Mary have specialized in this obscure art. From Egypt to Greece, to Persia, to the Arab peninsula and the Western world, all have fallen under its spell, offering riches beyond dreams. But are these material or spiritual? Some denounce one in favour of the other, some allude to both. Ploughing through this morass of obfuscation, it occurred to me that only a holistic view could prevail, and so nothing was excluded. As above So below; it seemed an appropriate maxim for all and nothing. Hermetisists have for millennia equated their Master and Guide, Hermes Trismegistus, a Graeco-Egyptian philosopher with Thoth, who was known to have written 42 books on the principles of Nature, in which strong metaphor disguises the true esoteric value, protecting the sacred from the profane:

> "Tis true, without falsehood, and most real: that which is above is like that which is below, to perpetrate the miracles of the One thing. And as all things have been derived from One, by the thought of One, so all things are born from this thing, by adoption. The Sun is its Father; the Moon is its Mother. Wind has carried it in its belly; the Earth is its Nurse. Here is the Father of every perfection in the world. His strength and power are absolute when changed into Earth: thou wilt separate the Earth from the fire, the subtle from the gross, gently and with care. It ascends from Earth to Heaven, and descends again to Earth to receive the power of the superior and inferior things. By this means, thou wilt have the glory of the world. And because of this, all obscurity will flee from thee. Within this is the power, most powerful of all powers. For it overcome all subtle things, and penetrate every solid thing. Thus the world was created. From this will be, and will emerge, admirable adaptations of which the means are here. And for this reason, I am called Hermes Trismegistus, having the three parts of the philosophy of the world. What I have said of the Sun's operations is accomplished"[184]

This beautiful process expresses how the body becomes 'transformed' into a body of light, emitting an ethereal glow, where the body is said to 'shine like the Sun, as gold'. Transmutation of base metals into gold as a literal act was accompanied by another, of greater value – that of the sojourn of the soul through seven progressive stages of alchemy, a process of sublime blessedness. Union of heart and intellect, soul and mind within the divine ennobles the soul, procures ascension to Godhead, commonly perceived as the 8th stage, linking it to the ascent upon the *'Otz Chim'* (Tree of Life). Gold was linked to the Sun, the mediator (halfway) between Earth and the Supreme.

The primary ingredient for alchemical work is *'prima materia,'* the visible and invisible substance of creation. Medieval alchemists combined their labour/work (labor) with their practise and place of prayer (*oratorium*), making no distinction as we do now in the 21st century, producing the laboratorium, a far cry from the cold, sterile clinic of modern scientists. The first (of seven) stages of alchemy is Putrefaction/decay, relating to the dross matter of the flesh and its removal from bone to reveal the 'true heart of the matter,' a metaphor for the destruction of bodily passions and desires that impede the full progress of the soul, trapped within.

> "The sages say that a wild beast is the forest,
>
> Whose skin is of blackest dye.
>
> If any man cut off his head,
>
> His blackness will disappear
>
> And give place to a snowy white."

Seeds blossom from the putrefied flesh, into eternal life without blemish. There can be no life without death, no salvation without redemption. Clearly, man must descend into the darkness of the grave, into the depths, the abyss before he can ascend to the eternal clarity of light. A charming allegorical medieval woodcut depicts a hopeful corpse, raising his head to heaven as a black raven separates his flesh from his bones, as this happens, his soul and mind, two small white birds leave the body with the last breath to become angels.

Completion of the work inculcates a state of 'being' beyond 'knowing.' A symbol of this never-ending premise is the Ouroboros, also a circuit for molecular change. From the 12th century, alchemists stressed the need for the philosopher's stone, a magical gem capable of transmuting the physical and the metaphysical; descriptions of a black or white stone suggest a pearl or meteorite in which all colours are unified within. Considering that no one had yet split the prism, and were therefore unaware of the unity of light within both black and white, this is an amazing testament. It is of immense significance. Kyphi is mentioned as a fabled Egyptian meteoric stone of which the incense named after it is contrived to resemble it. The four elements plus the fifth – spirit formed the *'Quintessence,'* permeating all that is omnipresent in its desire to be free of its material prison. Silence and secrecy are pre-requisites for success.

This initiatory journey of the soul passing from matter to spirit is poetically allegorised through purification by baptism, which facilitates Mystical Union, or the Gnostic sacrament of the 'Bridal Chamber,' a divine union *('Unio Mystica')* between the self and an angelic spirit of God. The divine and perfect androgyne is formed when this 'marriage' of the Sun and the Moon generates the 'seed' (the mysterious philosopher's stone) of their union, resulting from their unifying embrace within or in front of a cave (the body of the alchemist). The stone produced becomes a 'catalyst' for others. Parallels are here apparent to

Eastern tantric systems, of Shakti and Shiva. Underpinning all of these is the axiom of unification.

Spiritual processes ensure the separation of the soul (which is always perceived as female/receptive, irrespective of gender) from the body, allegorised as the Father, who absorbs the Son (spirit) after its unification with the soul (bride through its marriage). Thus the body is transformed after the ascension of soul into spirit, where it encounters the 'superior.' Man's threefold essence of salt, sulphur and mercury reflect the threefold nature of the Universe: Father, Son and the Holy Spirit (that moves all) As above, so below:

- Salt is identified with the heavy Saturn, whose symbol of a black cube = the Body
- Sulphur is the yellow flame/torch of the Soul, and of Space = Female
- Mercury is the Matrix of the Spirit, Intellect and of Time, = Male

Thus the emblem of man's perfection is the divine androgyne (not in any way perceived as physical or sexual, but a purely spiritual state), the union of the soul (Shekinah) with spirit (God). The body does not become bisexual, asexual or physically hermaphroditic; this is true harmony, the pure being of a 'perfected soul,' a '*sahu*,' a 'catharii' etc. Misunderstanding of this esoteric mystery asserts an erroneous 'physical' androgyny that denies the highest mystery, the separate and distinct essences/powers of God, held in perfect balance and harmony. The magical element of Mercury represents perfection, expressed as a combination of fixed and volatile elements (Earth/matter/body plus ether/spirit). Alchemy is an occult philosophy that rationalises material transmutation. The sage or adept realises his/her illumination when all distinction of soul and spirit as manifest states ceases:

Pleroma: the spiritual plenitude of the divine world of light

Kenoma: the material void of the earthly world of phenomena

No conflict exists between faith and science. By careful study of a few select premises offered within the field of alchemy, we can begin to understand the process and purpose, albeit couched in arcane and metaphysical terminology:

- Time is represented by 12 Zodiac/constellations, months etc.
- There are 5 emblems within alchemy, to represent the stages of ascent: raven, swan, dragon, pelican and phoenix. [5 x 12 = 60]
- Man is Fire, Air, Gold, Lion and Sun
- Female is Earth, Water, Silver, Eagle and Moon.
- Fire is not Solar light, but Zodiacal light.
- Prima materia: World Soul, Sophia/Wisdom, primal essence, mother of all elements.
- Gnostic Trinity of Father, Mother and Son represent the union of Body and Spirit by the attainment of Wisdom, inspired and granted by Sophia, (the World Soul). This typifies the Micro/Macrocosm.
- Inspiration = 'in spirit', possession, a compact between artist and daemon. It is the other, the adversary, the Shaiton, the anti-self, the divine self – the mind/nous.
- 3 daemons preside over the body, soul and intellect (nous)
- Mind is (nous) the good daemon.
- Gnostics regarded the Serpent of wisdom as an avatar of the Divine Mind, they saw Seth, the 3rd son of Adam as the Agathodaemon, the Lion, Serpent/Sun and (father of Enoch/ Idris –Hermes Trismegistus). Seth gave the Sabaeans their faith.

The Soul has to be pure in order to ascend the ladder of grace, with Heart and Mind to be in total harmony, without conflict (love under will – evolove). These elements were portrayed as soul and spirit, separate and distinct from the body (matter); the process was one of surrender, a union of the highest love, a spiritual marriage, activated by transcending seven levels through four worlds. Perhaps we can now begin to place things into their context.

During the medieval period, these teachings were refined, and a visual aesthetic articulated this arcane lore. Primal and intellectual energies of Aphrodite and Hermes form the glyph of the 'hermaphroditic' principle. Extremes in ascetic life patterns or debauchery lead the soul to harmonic ascension upon the middle pillar. Indeed, 'mercurial' eloquence is in fact silence, for the quick silver tongue holds its council, a mystery understood by even the most notorious exponents of the occult; Crowley too it seems deferred to '*Harpocrates*,' the silent Horus. Crowley perceived the path of the lightening flash upon the Tree to be that of Silence. Expressed succinctly in the maxim: *'to will, to dare, to know and to be silent,'* occultists add - to evolve/evolove.

Silence of course refers to the phenomenal periphery, the revealed world of appearances, where experiences are inexpressible by common language. Moreover, this protects the sacred from the profane. Silence is the most arcane mode of transmission; as contemplation between the self and the divine it is a passive act of submission. True magical silence is creative; talk dissipates and disrupts the flow of congress. This is afforded by only two states wherein a total absence of thought and speech induces:

1. a dreamless sleep

    and

2. Samadhi of the highest (non-volitional) kind.

Mantra emulates the harmonics of the heavenly spheres signified by the bee, whose humming vibrates molecular activity in tune with that of the universe. Symbolic of the mysteries, bees bring the gift of wisdom or mystical manna, the divine elixir. So, it is clear that the seven stages of alchemy refer not literally from lead to gold, or even from Saturn to Sun, but from dross to purity, from dark to light, the ultimate light . . . the Universal Creatrix and Source. Of course, a paradox is suggested here, if we do not move from Saturn as lead to Sun as gold, and if the highest light is Zodiacal/Stellar Light, do we then presume that because we now know our Solar System is Heliocentric we should place the Sun in the middle of the planetary listings? If so, then the parallel system of the Kabbalah becomes sharply relevant. Remember that medieval Kabbalism is considered based upon an earlier Chaldean model of eight stages.

Saturn then is clearly the key, and its planetary representative of Set/Har reveals the Sun/Sirius duality. Set/Anubis = putrefaction or the corruption that heralds new life. This ancient reptile of the abyss is lauded by other names: Tiamat and Leviathan, denoting the primality of its qualities. These are symbolised in the twin serpents of the Caduceus of mercurial air, of mind and the spaces beyond the northern regions. 'Saturn is the Black Sun behind Sun/Son; the stellar father is hidden behind the solar son, the true and ultimate light of existence.'

Here the process shifts from Lead/Saturn to Gold/Sun, from Carbon to Diamond, which also reads as Malkuth to Kether - Saturn to Saturn of a higher octave. Yet may we equate this metaphor of the transformation of base matter into pure light, of carbon to diamond, of Earth to Saturn, Malkuth to Kether? Does this relate to the adamantine body and the aspiration into the pure crystalline form of Buddha hood? The Sun/Son unites all principles of time, eternity etc, through his Mediumship; he truly is the centre of our 'Universe'. We can assert a similar and cumulative correlation with the four worlds of the Kabbalah through the elements, compass points, symbols and processes of the four stages of the alchemical process:

Element	World/level	Process	Compass	Symbol
Earth	Assiah	blackening	south	raven
Air	Yetzirah	whitening	north	peacock
Water	Briah	yellowing	west	swan
Fire	Aziluth	reddening	east	phoenix

Before this work may be undertaken, a person is first advised to pass through the 12 gates of the Zodiac (March to March) to become pure and properly prepared, there to commence the 'Great Work'. Metaphorically termed a 'red stone,' an apprentice is now ready to attempt the seven true stages that render him a 'lapiz' – the *'lapis exilis,'* the true 'gold' of the philosophers' stone - the 'Grail' of gnosis. The principles of gold and silver (Sun and Moon) unite to form the lapiz the 'philosophical' (not elemental Mercury) – named Azothe. A 'ladder' of seven rungs leads the apprentice through his ascension towards this individual and experiential gnosis where the dual essence of Mercury is represented by the crowned genius or Azothe (Virtue).

The traditional glyph for this is of a virile young man holding in each hand a caduceus, opposing male fencers wield a young eagle (*Nekhbet*) and a crowned snake (*Uraeus,*) symbolic of the male and female essences, fixed and volatile. Dissolved in mercurial water by Azothe, the stone or 1st matter is fermented and heated, until it changes colour to become gold, thereafter the *'lapis exilis'* or fusion of aspiration. *'Solve et coagula'* occurs after the dissolution and final union of the red/male/lion with the white female unicorn. Other symbols of divine androgyny are: serpent; dragon; phoenix, and within the occult world – Baphomet: Ass as the Set animal and woman combine. Together now as 'one,' spirit and soul begin their shift upwards through the 'elemental realms'; beginning with Saturn, where subjective linear time morphs into '*kairos*' (god's time in accordance with Fate).

Beginning in the optimum season, given as Spring, the mystic surrenders 9 months, hoping to achieve their goal around the Winter Solstice. It has been suggested that the soul of the dead is assimilated to the progress of the stars typified by Sirius, born again of the Mother Nuit in the eastern sky after its disappearance in the west. Superficially, at least, this follows the course of the Sun, given in The Orion Mystery as:

> "…the dead person's soul yet to be reborn enters the 'Duat', is gestated within the womb of Nuit, to be reborn when the star rises in the east for its helical rising 70 days later." However, this simple explanation of the stars 'apparent', motion ignores the star's meridian rise, transit, and setting, which is claimed to take 70, 120 and 90 days respectively…this equals a total of 280 days, exactly the same [average] time for human gestation."[185]

Bauval uses this information to prove a belief in re-incarnation, which it may, but the real value of this information is how it stresses and preserves the esoteric synthesis of stellar and solar core concepts. Within alchemy, the term INRI means: Igne Naturae Renovatur Integra (Nature, by fire is renewed in its integrity,) which is a curious enigmatic metaphor for purification!

But it can also mean: Yud; Nun; Resh; Yud = Fire, Water, Air and Earth – expressed as:

Yud	divine masculinity
He	divine femininity
Vau	physical masculinity
He	physical femininity

Hermeticism, a syncretism of Gnostic, Neo-Platonism and Sabaean

(Chaldean) star lore, expresses the universal pulsation of desire and attraction. Beauty is exalted as Phanes Protogenus, the golden winged angel, or Eros, the first-born revealer. As the Gnostic saviour God, he is recognised by the formulae IAO. Love/Eros conjoins the higher and lower powers by marrying the noumenal and phenomenal realms into a transcendent synthesis, bound by and in accordance with the 'golden chain' of sympathetic correspondences.[186] Knowledge of this process of synthemata is crucial for successful transmutation of the soul and talismanic theurgy:

> " if you know my word, you may make Heaven descend upon Earth, so that it may abide in you", the Earth which rises to heaven is that which hears the voice of wisdom, which has ceased to be a terrestrial spirit and has become celestial – this is the 'Great Work' of Holy Magic." [187]

The '*Quinta essentia*,' or celestial substance, becomes resolved when the elements are cross-polarised, made manifestation within the compass Mandala, uniting all correspondences, reified and bound within the 5th - the sacred omphalos, the nux, centre and axis mundi.

> "The One is all things and no one of them; the divine juggler brings the phenomenal cosmos into existence, and who sustains them, assuming all shapes and forms whilst remaining essentially changeless itself." Plotinus

> "All things were by the contemplation of the One, so all things arose from the One, by a single act of adaptation."
> Hermes Trismegistus

The circle is closed when the 'seven have become one'. That is when the alchemy has '*fused*,' all magics are complete, the communion blessed, sanctified and consumed, the union bridged – bliss achieved. (*Robert*

Cochrane of course mentioned this enigmatic statement in several of his letters.) Jacob Boheme expresses this mystery sublimely:

> "The curse of God has entered the seven figures, so they are in conflict with one another. Just as the human will was transformed into eternal Sun, calm in God, so in the philosophical work must all figures be transformed into One, into Sol. From seven must come One, and yet it remains in seven, but in one desire, as every figure desires the others in love, so there is no longer any conflict."

CLAN INSIGNIA

The Poison Chalice

Philosophy is a 'preparation for death' – it teaches the soul, once free of the body, how to maintain itself in the great hereafter, the sentient world of a true reality; and also how to avoid re-incarnation. Here the requisite knowledge is attained on the hylic plane where blindly we grope as flesh, mourning the amnesiacs cup. Frail memory traces disperse within the Waters of the Lethe. Our potentiality for advantageous progress, for evolution awakens and stirs the fires of these primal desires, our yearning to be free, to find the bliss of that poignant reality, the embrace of which lures us ever closer to itself.

The self (*Purusha*) is but a stranger to (*Prakriti*), the world of forms, traversing the drama of its own existence as a spectator. The soul sleeps until reawakened. Sleep (*Hypnos*) is brother to death (*Thanatos*). Metaphorical language describes the ignorance, captivity and intoxication as 'sleep' of a spiritual death. Victory over such states is sought through initiatic ordeal, triggering anamnesis. The Vigil inspires the aspirant to wakefulness suppressing the sleepful ignorance. Consciousness defeats the fatigue of the soul, just as stamina overcomes fatigue of the flesh.

"Awake from the slumber of drunkenness into which thou hast fallen."

Human perfection is conceived of as an unbroken unity within the divine androgyny – the state of being that denies all polarity, all duality and all separation. Baptism allows the recovery of the primordial condition of the divine androgyny. The wise spirit has encompassed its realised soul, fusing the harmonic of ascent and release. Mytho-geographic eschathologies generate celestial havens of respite, half-way dreamlands peopled by poets and visionaries, whose insightful projections, paved the way for those wandering pilgrims to follow in their wake.

It is said that they who behold the beauty of the world begin to stimulate the production of wings, sprouting forth, unfurling gently, taking flight towards gnosis, illuminated by the spiral updraft of Wisdom's own breath. A seeker who embraces the Tao is one who comprehends their wings. *"Intelligence is the swiftest of birds."* Gnosticism espouses the Fate of mankind within its 'doctrine of return'; freedom lies in the overcoming of this 'fate' through surrender to the Highest Will. The 'shining light' or Xvarenah of divinity is consubstantial with the epiphany of Grace, imparted during the phenomenology of dedication. Such ecstasies are discovered within the copious writings of the great mystics of all ages, whose singular vision has attracted us by their example. Historical Gnosticism hails from a pure source far older than the heretical cult named by the 1-2nd century polemical texts, and is heir to messianic traditions of avatars, mystical lore, angelic tutelage and Merkavah mysteries, maintained by oral teaching through a mentoring system centred in the individual. Beginning as apprentices, the aspirant evolves into one who progresses towards and finally achieves the title of *'Perfectii.'*

A document in Rome concerning the Arian heresy, associates Christ with the Archangel Michael as a servant of the Light. Orphic, Vedic and Platonic ideologies syncretise to form a unique perspective of the nature of the divine and how we, as aspects of it should approach it. Platonic concepts maintain the demi-urge as lacking in evil, whose creation of the manifest world as a harmonic is to be enjoyed. The 'fall' according to Plotinus is merely the voluntary descent of spirit to elevate the hylic matter consigned beneath the arc of heaven, above which the stars are the celestial repositories of divine energy. The incarnating soul loses its 'plenitude' and autonomy, becoming subject to Fate, mortality and existence. Aeonic totality constitutes the world seeded by the core of primordial spirit.

Helen and Simon Magus conjoin in myth to replicate the union of the lover and the beloved. Creation resulted from Sophia's desire to know herself as form, and to know God in that form – her descent inculcated the myth of the Gnostic redeemer, who slowly draws her back into himself, aided by the faith of all 'fragments' of her splintered soul, seeking liberation first of themselves, then of all. Three classes of the faithful exist:

1. Pneumatics - enlightened souls (guaranteed salvation through attainment)

2. Psychics - aware souls (have ignited souls so may be drawn back with assistance as they lack in spiritual guidance)

3. Hylics - material form still in ignorance (somatics immersed in carnality, doomed to disappear)

According to myth, when all attain pneuma, then all will ascend and the illusory world of Maya will be annihilated. Valentinian Gnosticism asserts salvation through gnosis for all. Libertine elitists believe the work is achieved through disregard for cultural mores designed for those who have not surrendered to their spiritual will for true guidance. The Rishis and Yogins share this elitist perspective, asserting it as one of inspired inheritance. The discovery of the light body, of the divine self – the atman, or higher guardian angel, is analogous to the Iranian concept of the celestial transcendent image of the soul. Philosophers have long hypothesised that our salvation lies not in the actuality of our divinity, but in its belief. Hidden within the Mind's Jewel (pineal gland) is the seat of Wisdom, requiring activation from the Poison Chalice, the moment of surrender and of sacrifice- the double tau, given artistic expression in the 'Cross of Lorraine', which is also known as the cross of poisoners. St John is witness to this divine cup.

Yet mankind is inexorably linked to the shift from cosmic titanic forces to those of mediation inducing greater sentience of the individual. This metaphysical separation is the 'fall,' the rent in the fabric of consciousness. Complex creation myths commonly attempt to allegorise the evolution of the self as the struggle between Khaos and Order, each concept spawning distinct pantheons of gods and heroes who engage in the eternal battle for the 'souls' of mankind. The soul is of course the ego, the awareness of the 'I' singularity. Mystics therefore seek its dissolution and integration, not as individuation but in the process of apotheosis. We are all gods in the truest sense that we are all of God.

Sufi mystic Ibn 'Arabi wrote poignantly of the One reality, of Haq or Truth and of the wisdom to attain it acquired by ascension of *'Tûbâ'* the Celestial Tree of Paradise, whose roots are paradoxically connected to its poisonous twin *'Zaqqûm'*. He explains poetically how both are fed from the same source, the choice being of man's own Fate – a cup offered equally to all, such that some will be nourished by wisdom, others the torment of ignorance.[188] Robert Cochrane wrote insightfully of this mystery:

> "We are still babes suckling at the breast whose milk is poisonous, yet we think that we flourish upon poison. Truth no matter how we interpret it feeds demons as well as Saints"[189]

Teresa of Avila, supreme mystic and visionary similarly commented upon the Beloved's Gift - the 'milk' that nourishes us from Her Breast:

"The soul is like an infant still at its mothers breast: such is the mother's care ... the will simply loves, and no effort needs to be made by the understanding, for it is the Lord's pleasure that, without exercising its thought, the soul should realise that it is His company, and should merely drink the milk which His Majesty puts into its mouth and enjoy its sweetness.[190]

Therefore it becomes clear that a materialistic origin for the gods, for creation, for the fall et cetera, becomes an irrelevant distraction from 'the work', which is simply to understand that the process exists and to evolve we must embrace the teachings within the mysteries that will restore our Edinic status. This 'salvation' or 'redemption' has no religious connotations, no espousal of negative doctrines, no fear of consequence; rather it offers methodical focus towards the re-unification of the primal bliss: the pleroma, a serene state of awareness of uncompromising totality.

Oneiric experiences enhance progress of requisite apprehension, wherein the seeker desires Moksha, the freedom from profane beliefs, rather than existence, which is a natural condition and should not be despised as some early and extreme Gnostic sects have done. The 'death' experience has thus been explored to better understand this precarious relationship between existence and the 'I.' Gnosis gained through familiarity of the primordial states facilitate the development of cosmologies and eschathologies, which serve as maps to guide the pilgrim through uncertain and unpredictable landscapes. Intriguingly, these maps are invariably based in cultural perspectives, bearing specific keys to the world view of each tribe, cult, people or nation.

For example, the followers of Orphism professed hereditary succession of the legendary 'Kabiri,' who as 'divine' craftsmen were metallurgists, smiths, healers and holy men. Association to this ancestral legacy defined for them the guidance and protection of archaic forces of the sea and land that had 'shaped' the world through their unification by 'spirit,' perceived as the winds or air. Pre-Gnostic Orphism had pronounced extreme asceticism focussed upon renunciation of that Promethean world, which though enlightened, had inadvertently incurred the wrath of the gods, perceived as wrathful 'Fate.' Nemesis was the balancing force they sought to assuage and master through their aspirative devotions.

Divine twins as opposing discarnate and incarnate idioms generated the core of the Orphic Mysteries, attracting many initiates across the ancient world. Temples allegedly dedicated to the eponymous deities of these profound mysteries are speculated to have twin pillars within their construction dedicated to the divine 'twins' who are concatenate with similar myths of Prometheus and Cadmus as progenitors and mediators in mankind's evolution. The establishment of such ancestry was deemed essential for correct understanding of the mysteries and for acceptance into them, especially through ancestral mediation, without which the soul was lost on its quest.

Orpheus is the deity most frequently connected with Orphic cultus, albeit more specifically of divine prophecy, through the oracular head. Numerous deities, from Inanna to Jesus are expounded in the greatest of myths to have endured the process of *'katabasis,'* an underworld descent to specifically encounter alternate realities and to understand the mysteries of life and death. Other deities who became subject to this egress also share significant correlations within the Luciferian schema; Castor & Pollux, Lazarus, Hu-Asar (Osiris); Gilgamesh; Baldr; Dionysus; Tammuz; Hermes, Orpheus and Psyche.

In contra-distinction to this process, *'katharsis'* induces the highly charged emotional purge, the *'orgia,'* the act of sensorium, or extreme indulgence. This therionic frenzy of uncensored expression propels the mind into khaos, aggressively forcing suppressed anxieties or emotions to surface, where they are literally expunged through this very act that violates order. Dionysus is hailed as the supreme god-force associated with this rampant hysteria, of ecstasy in the truest sense of surrender of intellect to raw passion, where 'Mind' is placed beyond emotive experience, and the consumed body quivers with exultant effulgence. Participants suffering from various neuroses either witting or otherwise, achieve balance through vicarious submission to psycho-drama.

Both extremes have and still continue to form the basis of the mysteries to varying degrees, whereupon the seeker loses first the identity, then the sense of separation, before finding the unity of being at the soul level. Gnosis of this encourages and supports the individual then through life as we each make our way towards the greater ingress, confident in the 'reality' of it. That later Gnostics of the 5th and 6th centuries became tragically polluted by the destructive influences of Manichaean extremism, whose irrational pessimisms and dualistic doctrines espouse the denial of matter, should not prevent us from returning to a less inhibited and more embracing Truth. In fact the mysteries retain the keys of anamnesis to address the topical issues of societal imbalance, soteriological indoctrination and the dearth of existential solace.

Even so, Saturn is the Muse of Solitude, and thus each pilgrim's path is walked alone, finding only occasional respite in companie. Here we cogitate the *'via unitiva'* our individual longing for God, expressed through aspirative prayer, devotion and inner alchemy. Of such mysteries, Augustine said:

"Man may say nothing of what he is incapable of feeling, but
he can feel what he is incapable of putting into words."

Initiatic traditions retain the mystery of the Grail quest. Often presented obliquely, the seeker is encouraged to attain the sacred 'draught of immortality,' the precious pearl of gnosis and profound elixir of inner alchemy. Archaic myth refers to the Grail as *'Haoma'* or *'Soma,'* being Eucharistic in nature. By consumption of the holy essence, we are ourselves transcendent. Both Haoma and Soma are terms which relate equally to deities aligned to these enigmatic mysteries, linking them to the Orphic and Dionysian rites in which 'god-eating' was requisite.

But even though the *'Grail'* concept has evolved, shifting away from violent and extrovert displays of hysteria, the rationale remains intact. It is often assumed that those early savage and bloody rites were no more than acts of defiance, a rebellion against the austerities of the archaic world. This may of course be true. Yet there is more. Glimpses into the multifarious practises of mystics hint towards a deeper purpose, so fundamental the terms are so abstruse, so veiled we speak through poetic metaphor, with reverence and with awe. Language both evokes and guards against its revelation. The Grail becomes the chalice; the draught of immortality becomes the poisoned elixir; the rite becomes that of the Poison Chalice.

> "One flash of Your cup, and the next moment
> I'm pouring wine for prostitutes and madmen.
> One glimpse of Your lightening Crown,
> *I'm dancing headless."*[91]

But what does this mean? Certainly, the quest is one of discovery, of reclaiming that which has been lost, of salvation. Its restoration signifies a return to a blessed state, before the 'fall', whence man enjoyed a primal purity among the gods. We have essentially 'lost' Paradise and yearn to walk unharmed through the flaming sword that bars our return. The destiny of a people remains tied to 'Fate,' that challenges the Grail seeker to discover truth through adversity, a battle engaged with profane abstraction to gain gnosis of 'eternity,' or more properly, the 'sense of eternity' which is the restoration of all tradition.

This is the egregore of its people, it spiritual life-blood and identity. Dionysus, god of ecstasy, is renowned for his 'drunken' revels. But his mysteries of sublime intoxication reveal an authentic initiatic expression of inner esoterica. Hebrew language awards the same value to both *'yayin'* for wine and *'sod'* for mystery and this is in full accord with the esoteric tradition of the Sufis who consider wine a metaphor for the most holy wisdom; particularly with regard to the all consuming addiction to that sweet draught of poison imparted by the divine Sophia, from whose lips the 'kiss of the beloved' bestows fervent love-longing into the sacred cup of gnosis. Lost in such blind destructive oblivion, this potent beverage is reserved only for those whose palate has been duly prepared – the elect, or elite, those who tread the initiatic path of annihilation; submission in true awareness.[192]

> "Eternity waits behind the transparent door
> Of each moment. Love the Beloved, and that door
> Swings open: Eternity enters, pouring the wine
> *No-one who drinks can ever recover from.*"[193]

Wine from such a cup, intoxicates the yearning Soul, transporting it, enraptured into the sublime realms of 'immortality,' where Time ceases its vulgar passage, and Haq, divine Truth shines forth hidden illumination upon the drunkard, heady with their revelation. Curiously, 'Haq' is easily transposed to *'Chockmah,'* Wisdom of the Kabbalah. She carries the light or virtue of *'kan'* becoming manifest as *'qan,'* from which we derive Qain, or 'leader' and Kingdom. The dwelling place of this supreme emissary of virtue, the Shekinah is the Holy Mountain, the High place (Malkuth) which equates with the primordial Eden. And this is where it must be claimed.[194]

"I drank the filter of Your passion
O Water of life – I drank, and became You.
Death came, and smelled Your fragrance all over me
Death himself grew drunk and forgot to kill."[195]

Paracelsus expresses this in equally enigmatic alchemical terms:

"He who wants to enter the divine realm, first must enter his mother's body, and die herein."

'Rectificando' in the middle of the acronym VITRIOLUM means 'to put right,' to reinstate the true nature, the purification of that which is deemed negative or undesirable. It is to straighten all that has grown crooked during our lives. The alchemist must purify himself of all 'dross' inimical to evolution. Descent to the root within, in like manner of Orpheus, Tammuz and Osiris. To partake of the essence from the 'Tree of Life' is to draw in equal measure the essence of 'Death' and She must be embraced as a lover. But this is not bodily death. Her gnosis is the kiss of death only to the ego self for the reinstatement of the divine soul. The Covenant of Resurrection is the Manna, Haoma, and Soma, the golden elixir of all inner mysteries. There can be no transformation without this death of the self, surrendered to Her within the acceptance of the fate surrendered in the Eucharist of the Poison Chalice. Where both become -as-one: the realised soul.

Within the science of vegetal alchemy, that which cures may also kill. In surrender, Fate decides. Will She inflame with Her divine madness, transforming you forever, an immortal among Her 'darling crew' or will She reject you to become a member of the 'dead'? Her celestial 'dew' is that glorious state, of trance-formation, inducting the elevation of the fallen, restoring the self to its own divinity. The aspirant's mortality hangs in the balance, poised upon the brink of true immortality. And here we are returned to the 'philosopher's stone', the draught of immortality, the '*Vitriolum*' – true medicine of the Poison Chalice.

POISONED CHALICE [AFTER JOHN]

Epilogue:

In all matters of life and death we are ever subject to the equilibrating ambivalence of Her Law. This is to paraphrase Robert Cochrane, to follow Truth by giving up all illusion, to face what may be the greatest illusion of all. This is the basis of the 'Faith' and the Faith is subject to Her Law.

THE LAW:

"Do not do what you desire,	1
Do what is necessary,	2
Take all you are given-	3
Give all of yourself.	4
What I have, I hold.	5
When all else is lost, And not until then,	6
Prepare to die with dignity."	7

(Robert Cochrane)

He goes on to explain, very briefly how to view them:

"The first is perhaps one of the most difficult criterions to live by – since there is no room for illusion. The second allows you little time for yourself, the third is the keystone of wisdom and the fourth is the basic key to the witch personality."

Further analysis of this fundamental Seven-Fold 'Law' yields quite profound considerations. My own understanding of it is by no means comprehensive, but it is drawn from inspiration within the Clan. The depth of it is legion.

1 Desire is of course about gratification. It is about the sensuous delights of life itself. It is completely subjective. It alludes to illusion.

2 Necessity is the harsh, biting reality, the unrelenting tide of 'fate'. This wave of assault forces the hand to act in accord with the will aligned to the external demands of duty, of sacrifice, of non-subjective causes.

3 Holding all that is given concerns the ability to receive. Giving is easy enough. How many of us can take? In taking we acknowledge the bond twixt giver and receiver and recognize the value of sharing gifts, though not ones of material worth. They are of great value and must be nurtured in faith; preserved by discretion; and hallowed in awe.

4 Giving of the self in return is the surrender of 'will,' rightly asserted as not being 'virtue.' The will is an impediment to true sight and is given up. Removal of this obstacle is the giving of the 'all' - the self as a blank canvas for the virtue, as yet untapped within, to be stimulated by the teacher without.

5 This mentor keeps all for himself, that is to say, his gnosis is his own, it is of no use to the next man who cannot walk in his shoes. It is held by him as his guide and key to the next level of his/her own evolution. The mentor instils many things within

his student, but never his own argosy. Wyrd is an individual tone.

6 When one lose sight of the truth, loses the way to it or abandons it, then this person is 'lost', literally and figuratively. Without Truth, there is no hope, no understanding and no purpose in this life given to discover the profound secrets of these things.

7 This brings us to the reason for death. Without purpose, 'The Faith' is dead. Without vigour in life, virtue wanes. So life loses its hold and we slip into stasis, the cold grip of death. It beckons us towards another life, another role through which to fulfil the ideals we lost in this one. And so, only then do we choose when and how such a death is acquired. The appointment is arranged by the context and according to the dictates of circumstance. No-one else decides this point in time, but ourselves.

And as this tome draws to a close, a moment's pause perhaps on the 'fallen' be they angels, kings, priests or men – for in the immortal words of Robert Cochrane are not *"the Hunter the Hunted (Old Tubal Cain) and the Roebuck in the thicket, are one and the same divine presence. This **is** the time of the God of the mysteries- the Star-Crossed Serpent !"*

> *'Here be I stripped of all finery,*
> No clothes have I, excepting by thy Grace.
> Master, I have descended the path towards thy gates
> Leaving all but my truthful spirit behind me.
> Here I am as naked as the sea, as the sky, as the grave itself.
> I pray thee take pity on me and listen to my prayer.'

In life and death, we are the stars woven into the fabric of Wyrd; wide She casts Her net to catch the 'fallen,' to gather them up home again.

Robin-the-Dart

Notes

1 Sacred enclosure surrounding an ancient tree, marked for its prominence, and often at boundaries.
2 Norman Iles *'Who really killed Cock Robin?: Nursery Rhymes and Carols restored to their original meaning.'* 1986 Robert Hale Pub.
3 Norman Iles *'Who really killed Cock Robin?: Nursery Rhymes and Carols restored to their original meaning.'* 1986 Robert Hale Pub.
4 www.hedgewytchery.com/songs_chants.html
5 www.plexoft.com/SBF/green.grow.html
6 Joseph B. Wilson archive, courtesy of Stuart Inman, Doyen and Guardian of 1734 [private corress]
7 www.hymnsandcarolsofchristmas.com/... green_grow_the_rushes.html
8 www.plexoft.com/SBF/green.grow.html
9 B. Bettelheim. *'The Uses of Enchantment: Meaning and Importance of Fairy Tales'* 1976 London, pp54
10 www.digital.library.unt.edu/permalink/meta-dc-3694:1
11 F. Laroque. *'Shakespeare's Festive World'* 1993 Cambridge, p24
12 C. S. Burne. *'The Handbook of Folklore'* 1996 London, p350
13 R. Palmer. *'Britain's Living Folklore'* 1995 Felinfach, p48
14 *(ibid.)*
15 E. & M. A. Radford. *'Ency. of Superstitions'* 1974 GB, p28
16 E. & M. A. Radford. p101
17 R. Palmer. p57

18   R. Palmer. p58

19   R. Muchembled. *'A History of the Devil from the Middle-Ages to the Present'* 2003 UK, p15

20   M. Jurich. *'Scheherazade Sisters: Trickster Heroines'* 1998 Westport, p51

21   R. Muchembled. p115

22   M. Jurich. p51

23   B. Bettelheim. p312

24   F. Laroque. *'Shakespeare's Festive World'* 1993 Cambridge, p26 from the French - Arlecchino, once a terrifying figure who lead the souls of the damned, as recorded in the 11th century *'Ordericas Vitalis'* by a very pious monk!

25   F. Laroque. p26 & www.scribd.com/doc/2396347/The-Flourishing-of-Romance-and-the-Rise-of-AllegoryPeriods-of-European-Literature pp110-11

26   M. Jurich. p2

27   M. Jurich. p7

28   E. & M. A. Radford. *'Ency. of Superstitions'* 1974 GB, p188

29   E. & M. A. Radford p168

30   Readers Digest Ass. (Ed.) *'Folklore, Myths and Legends'* 1974 GB, p70

31   J.B. Russell. *'The Devil'* 1987 USA, p11

32   C. Larner. *'Witchcraft and Religion'* 1986 Oxford, p54

33   C. Larner. p136

34   E.J. Jones & Mike Howard (Ed.) *'The Robert Cochrane Letters'* 2002 Berks, p124

35   D. Valiente. *'ABC of Witchcraft'* 1984 London, pp 119-20

Suzerainty refers to the feudal relationship that exists in tribal societies and clans, where fealty secures protection by the liege lord and his tutelary god. This is unlike sovereignty where a monarch may be acknowledged, but no vassalage, duty or fealty is claimed by them nor surrendered to them.

36 (*Ibid.*) These are the two surviving language groups: P-Brythonic (Cornwall, Wales & Breton) and Q- Goidelic (Ireland, Scotland & Isle of Man).

37 D. Valiente. p129

38 Russell, p189

39 J. Harte. *'Explore Fairy Traditions'* 2004 UK, p23

40 J. Harte. *'Explore Fairy Traditions'* 2004 UK, p66

41 J. Harte. p40

42 J. Harte. p24

43 A. Porteous. *'Folklore of the Forest'* 1996 UK,p285

44 www.sacredtexts.com/cdshop/indexhtm chapter 13 *Etins are an older race of demi-gods, believed to exhibit magical prowess, often compared to the Indian Asuras because both groups of beings 'battled' against the gods.*

45 www.sacredtexts.com/cdshop/indexhtm chapter 13

46 J. Harte. *'Explore Fairy Traditions'* 2004 UK, p23; p86; p104; p124 and p148

47 J. Harte. p150/1 Teind is a tithe specifically of land produce

48 J. Harte. p150 and p128

49 E.J. Jones. *'Sacred Mask, Sacred Dance'* 1997 USA, p161-2

50 J. Harte. *'Explore Fairy Traditions'* 2004 UK, p50

51 R. Whitlock. *'Guide to British Folklore'* 1979 Oxford, p22

52 E.J. Jones. *'The Roebuck in the Thicket'* 2001 Berks, p112

53. R. Palmer. *'Britain's Living Folklore'* 1995 Felinfach, p18

54. Readers Digest Ass. (Ed.) *'Folklore, Myths and Legends'* 1974 GB, p72

55. C. Larner. *'Witchcraft and Religion'* 1986 Oxford, p151

56. D. Valiente. *'ABC of Witchcraft'* 1984 London, p204

57. R. Muchembled. *'A History of the Devil from the Middle-Ages to the Present'* 2003 UK p157

58. G&F Doel. *'Mumming, Howling and Hoodening'* 1992 Kent, p3

59. D. Valiente. p163

60. D. Valiente. p204

61. P.J. Awn. *'Satan's Tragedy and Redemption'* 1983 p12

62. E.J. Jones. *'Sacred Mask, Sacred Dance'* 1997, USA p166

63. W.E. Liddell. & M. Howard (Ed.) *'The Pickinghill Papers'* 1994 Berks. p103

64. Prof. R. Hutton. *'The Triumph of the Moon'* 1999 Oxford p313

65. B. Bushaway. *'By Rite: Custom, Ceremony and Community in England 1700-1880'* 1982 Junction Books, London p112

66. (*ibid.*)

67. C. Hole. *'British Folk Customs'* 1976 London, p127. *Significant now as Armistice Day, where we remember those fallen in death during the two world wars.*

68. Readers Digest Ass. (Ed.) *'Folklore, Myths and Legends'* 1974 GB, p462

69. D. Valiente. 1984 p248

70. D. Valiente. *'Witchcraft for Tomorrow'* 1985 London, p125

71. G. Ashe. *'Mythology of the British Isles'* 2002 London p106; 117; 123/4

72 S. Roud. *The English Year* 2008 England

73 Prof. R. Hutton. *The Triumph of the Moon* 1999 Oxford p232

74 J. Simpson *Legends of the Chanctonbury Ring* 1969 'Folklore' #80 pp122-131 *Simpson makes suggestions of decayed folk memory of ritual food or drink prepared by legendary priests for alternately their god or worshippers when processing this hill, probably due to the discovery in 1909 of the remains of a Romano-British temple, becoming fused with a more traditional theme, the most popular of which is the 'good folk'.*

75 J. Simpson & J Westwood. *The Lore of the Land* 2005 p728

76 Prof. R. Hutton. p307

77 D. Valiente. *Rebirth of Witchcraft* 1989 London p125

78 Readers Digest Association. (Ed.) *Folklore, Myths and Legends* 1974 GB p198/9

79 (Ibid)

80 www.feri.com/dawn/voluspa *Pagan Norse term from the Poetic 'Edda' that names the 'feris' as the dead souls that live underground.*

81 E. Maple. *'Cunning Murrell'* 1960 Folklore #71 pp36-43

82 J. Simpson & J Westwood. p723-9

83 Prof. R. Hutton. p104

84 *Both Evan John Jones and Doreen Valiente noted that the wife of the late Robert Cochrane was clearly the 'Sakti' and source of his power (pers. comm.).*

85 Prof. R. Hutton. p362

86 E.J. Jones & Mike Howard (Ed.) *The Robert Cochrane Letters* 2002 pp16-17, 21 & 51-3

87 Prof. R. Hutton. p81

88 Prof. R. Hutton. P91

89 Known as 'The Thames valley Coven'.

90 E. J. Jones (ed: Michael Howard)*'The Roebuck in the Thicket'* Capall Bann, 2001 p142

91 Doreen Valiente *'Rebirth of Witchcraft'* 1989 Robert Hale. UK p125

92 Count Eugene Goblet d'Alviella *'Symbols: Their Migration and Universality'* 2000 Dover NY p134

93 Jones, RitT. p53 *Here in his letter to the 'Pentagram' Magazine in 1965, Robert Cochrane expounds his view of the role of Fate in the game of life; the snake tempts and distracts, the ladder allows us to scale our will, transcending desire, in order to 'bind ourselves back' onto the path towards our destiny.*

94 Goblet d' Alviella p140-1

95 Goblet d' Alviella p144

96 John Williamson *'The Holly and the Oak Kings'* 1987 Harper Collins UK p100-1

97 Jones, RitT. p150

98 Raphael Patai *'The Hebrew Goddess'* 1990 Wayne state Uni Press p37 (*Asherah is also Ashratum, Ashtoreth, Astarte, Anath and Ishtar*)

99 G. R. Levy. *'The Gate of Horn'* 1953 Faber & Faber. London pp95-119

100 Goblet d' Alviella p159

101 Rene Guenon, *'Symbols of Sacred Science'* 2004 Sophia Perennis NY. P186

102 Levy, p120-1

103 Bayley, p193

104 Goblet d' Alviella p153

105 Goblet d' Alviella p189

106 Levy, p153

107 Levy, p200

108 As in 'religion'

109 Levy, p209

110 Harold Bayley, *The Lost Language of Symbolism*, 2006 Dover Pub. NY p269

111 D. Purkiss, '*A Witch in History*' 1996 Routledge UK p35

112 Bayley, p263

113 Levy, p241

114 E.J. Jones (ed: Michael Howard) '*Robert Cochrane Letters*' 2002 Capall Bann UK p181

115 Jones, RitT p134

116 Shani Oates '*The 4th Nail*'

117 E.J. Jones RCL p34

118 Levy, p168

119 Count Eugene Goblet d' Alviella, '*Symbols: Their Migration and Universality*' 2000 NY Dover Books p142

120 Goblet d'Alviella, p 236

121 *A sacred and holy tree, taking more common form as the Gospel Oak.*

122 Joseph Campbell, '*The Mythic Image*' 1974 MJF Books p266

123 *Essentially a sacred enclosure, or holy place, the stem root of garden, garnered, etc. In Norse language 'gardh' forms the principle syllable to the words, Asgardh, Midgardh and Utgardh, whose meaning indicates the central core/axis of Yggdrasil, the Cosmic world tree, having nine sacred enclosures orbiting its unifying trunk.*

124 Ibn 'Arabi '*The Tree of Being An Ode to the Perfect Man*' Interpreted

by Shaykh Tosun Bayrak al-Jerrahi al-Halveti 2005 Archetype, Cambridge pp142-143

125 Ibn 'Arabi pp 100-101
126 Jones, TRCL p143
127 Jones, RCL p142
128 Jones, RCL p92
129 Jones, RCL pp26-50
130 Shani Oates 'The Three Rings:' *Tubelo's Green Fire*. 2010 Mandrake Pubs UK pp238/9
131 Neville Drury & Stephen Skinner, *'The Search for Abraxas,'* 1972 Neville Spearman Ltd, London
132 Jones, RitT. p161
133 'Roses and Religion' by Sarah Coles: www.historicroses.org
134 Levy, p199
135 *This now famous 5,000 year old tree is said to mark the spot where Abraham entertained the three angelic visitors and the tent he raised for the 'presence' (Shekinah) of the Lord to dwell within.*
136 Bayley, 153
137 J. Roberts (ed) *'Oxford Dictionary of the Classical World.'* 2005. p220
138 Goblet d' Alviella p162
139 Goblet d' Alviella p169
140 Bayley, p310
141 Bayley, p356 Ig-dur-as-il, may be broken down and transliterated as: 'The great enduring light of God' (Flaming tree)
142 Joseph Campbell *'The Mythic Image'* 1974 MJF Books, NY. p260

143 J Robert (ed) *'Oxford Dictionary of the Classical World'* 2005 Oxford p220

144 *And as described by Cochrane as the correct way to greet the altar – Her as The Stang!*

145 Paula Marvelly, *'Women of Wisdom'* 2005 Watkins Publishing, London p84

146 Joseph Campbell *'The Mythic Image'* pp192-5

147 Campbell, p192

148 Metatron is possibly the Greek rendition of the Latin *metator*, meaning 'guide'

149 Jones, RCL p17

150 Jones, RCL pp92-93

151 Jones, RCL pp36-7

152 Bayley, p140

153 Dowson's Classical Dictionary of Hindu Mythology. http://www.mythfolklore.net/india/encyclopedia/varuna.htm]

154 Dr. W. Wagner *'Asgard and the Gods'* Routledge London.

155 *Robert Cochrane speaking of the element of sacrifice, the altar of perfumes upon which we offer the nafs to the self, the nephesch to the neschemah?* E. J. Jones *'The Robert Cochrane Letters'* Capall Bann.

156 Bayley, p259

157 Bayley, p263

158 http://en.wikipedia.org/wiki/Three-dimensional_space

159 http://en.wikipedia.org/wiki/Three-dimensional_space

160 Larissa Bonfante & Judith Swaddling *'Etruscan Myths'* British Museum Press UK 2006 p48

161 http://www.answers.com/topic/dimension

162 Paraphrase of Robert Cochrane's *'In Fate and the overcoming of Fate lies the Gail'*: www.cyberwitch.com/bowers/wilson

163 Bonfante & Swaddling p48

164 Lewis Spence *'The Mysteries of Britain'* 1994 Senate Paperbacks. UK p218 [Spring, Summer and Winter] *These are Cochrane's 'Three Elemental Queens' Arthur is the Wind God, Oak king, Tanist spouse to the heroic and eternal Lancelot d'lac.*

165 Jones, RCL p166-7

166 *Ibid.* p234

167 http://www.speakwithoutinterruption.com/site/2009/03/leadership/

168 http://www.speakwithoutinterruption.com/site/2009/03/leadership/

169 The seven flaming tongues of fire, who were the primal kalas, birthed by the effulgent Agni – the proto-type angels

170 Dowson's Classical Dictionary of Hindu Mythology http://www.mythfolklore.net/india/encyclopedia/varuna.htm

171 [*ibid.*]

172 [*ibid.*]

173 [*ibid.*]

174 Private correspondence - Ian Chambers 2-3-2010

175 *thing=assembly of Law; a sacred assembly and the enclave for it. Inductions are still held in those places in continuance of this practise.*

176 http://en.wikipedia.org/wiki/Norse_mythology

177 http://fmg.ac/Projects/MedLands/ENGLAND,%20AngloSaxon%2 0&%20Danish%20Kings.htm

178 http://en.wikipedia.org/wiki/Germanic_peoples

179 [*ibid.*]

180 [*ibid.*]

181 [*ibid.*]

182 Oates, pp160-1

183 *'Theosaurus Incantus: The Spagyric Quest of Beroaldus Cosmopolita'* Wyman & Sons. London

184 *The Emerald Tablet* http://www.templeofsolomon.org/Etablet.htg/emerald_tablet.htm

185 Robert Bauvall *'The Orion Mystery'* p221

186 Nigel Jackson. *'Celestial Magic'* Capall Bann Pub. 2003. UK p 41

188 Ibn 'Arabi, *The Tree of Being* 2005 Archetype. Cambridge. p106

189 Jones, p89

190 Paula Marvelly, *'Women of Wisdom'* 2005 Watkins Publishers, London p213

191 Andrew Harvey *'Rumi: Love's Glory'* Balthazar Books, San Francisco 1996

192 Rene Guenon *'King of the World'* Sophia Perennis Hillside NY pp32-3

193 Andrew Harvey *'Rumi: Love's Glory'* Balthazar Books, San Francisco 1996

194 Rene Guenon *'King of the World'* Sophia Perennis Hillside NY pp38-9

195 Andrew Harvey *'Rumi: Love's Glory'* Balthazar Books San Francisco 1996

Index

A

Abel 15, 33, 77, 136, 138, 139
Abraham 95, 97, 194
Abraxas 103, 194
Adam 37, 67, 69, 70, 77, 85, 94, 100, 111, 138, 139, 165
Adityas 86
Aegipan 7, 114, 117, 118
Agricultural 40, 41, 43, 129
Alchemy 7, 160, 164
Androgyne 163, 164
Anglo-Saxon 33, 40, 91, 111, 142
Anima Mundi 87, 103
Ankh 73, 83
Antahkarana 104
Asherim 67
Astarte 74, 192
Attis 70, 130
Awen 102, 111
Axis Mundi 66, 70, 82, 83, 87, 99, 103
Azothe 168

B

Bagabi Rune 43
Baphomet 119, 168
Beelzebub 29, 38
Beowulf 33
Beth-el 80
Black Goddess 123
Böötes 16
Boreas 17
Brahma 101, 108, 135, 136
Bronze Age 99

C

Cain 7, 9, 15, 16, 33, 40, 42, 77, 94, 109, 112, 114, 122, 129, 131, 132, 133, 134, 135, 136, 138, 139
Castor and Pollex 96
Cauldron 83, 117
Ceugent. 84
Chaldean 79, 167, 170
Chanctonbury Ring 43, 191
Clan of Tubal Cain 34, 35, 44, 46, 50, 55, 65, 70, 78, 139, 140, 145, 146, 147, 150, 154, 156
Cochrane, Robert 2, 11, 13, 15, 16, 18, 29, 39, 40, 47, 49, 50, 51, 52, 53, 54, 56, 59, 65, 66, 71, 83, 86, 89, 90, 91, 93, 103, 112, 125, 147, 148, 158, 171, 175, 183, 185, 188, 191, 192, 193, 195, 196
Cochranite 50
Cock Robin 15, 187
Compass 16, 58, 103, 108, 131, 137, 157, 159, 168
Crossed arrows 91, 93
Crucifixion 37, 98
Cunning Murrell 45, 191
Cunning-folk 36, 46, 47
Cylinder seal 69, 75

D

Devil 22, 28, 29, 38, 44, 77, 91, 119, 188, 190
  Divil 93, 99
Diabolist 24, 126
Diana 32, 96
Dionysus 2, 96, 102, 116, 118, 120, 136, 177, 178, 180
Dioscouroi 96
Divine Creatrix 75
Draco 16, 129, 132

Drighton 40, 119
Dumuzzi 79, 133

E
Eden 37, 70, 79, 87, 180
Egregore 7, 35, 46, 59, 66, 81, 103, 135, 140, 148, 152, 155, 156, 180
Elphame 30
Entheogens 28
Eve 67, 100

F
Faerie 22, 24, 27, 30, 31, 32, 34, 36, 37, 40, 42, 43, 44, 45, 48
Faith 7, 47, 48, 49, 52, 54, 58, 62, 63, 65, 89, 92, 101, 122, 150, 152, 165, 174, 183, 185
Faust 26, 27
Fealty 38, 39, 143, 150, 189
Feudalism 34, 40, 41, 148, 149, 189
Fey 27, 35
Fisher King 104, 151
Frau Gaude 103

G
Gardh 9, 87, 99, 143
Gardner, Gerald B 42
Gate of Horn 74, 79, 96, 192
Geis 107
Gills, Norman 51, 57, 62
Gnostic 60, 100, 153, 174
Gorgon 102
Gray, William G. (Bill Gray) 51, 55, 58
Green Grow the Rushes O. 13
Grendel 33, 119

H
Harpocrates 166
Heaven 14, 17, 19, 38, 73, 78, 79, 80, 84, 85, 92, 96, 97, 100, 102, 104, 105, 112, 161
Heimdall 143
Hekate 16, 66, 71, 83, 90, 96, 110, 119, 158
Hemlock 28
Herlekin 27
Hermaphrodite 93
Hermes 71, 86, 90, 96, 97, 98, 115, 118, 119, 120, 160, 161, 165, 166, 170, 177
Hieros Gamos 78, 132, 152
Holda 96, 111
Holy Cow 74
Horned God 93
Horse 89, 101
Horsemen 41, 110, 148
Howard, Michael 192, 193
Huginn 145
Hutton, Prof. R 40

I
Iamblichus 160
Inquisition 34

J
John Jones, E. 138

K
Kaaba 81
Kabbalism 84, 167
Khronos 130
Kundalini 99, 108

L
Lady of the Mountain 75, 84
Lammas 132
Lares 31
Law 18, 57, 65, 80, 147, 155, 183, 184, 196
Leukothea 7, 91, 114, 120, 121
Leviathan 167
Lily 102
Liminal 22, 31, 67, 92
Lucifer 32, 98, 135

M

Mabinogion 88
Magical argosy 49
Magister 35, 39, 46, 57, 66, 91, 93, 94, 147, 148, 155
Maleficarum 27, 29, 47
Martinmas 41
Martyrs 13
Maypole 69
Mays Eve 132
Maze 59
Metatron 102, 195
Michaelmas 38
Middle Ages 23, 31, 126, 149, 151
Midsummers Eve 44, 57
Midwinter 38
Moirai
 Fates. *See* atropos;clothos;lachesis
Mound 90, 97, 111, 119
Mummers 29, 38
Munnin 145
Muse 59, 118, 132, 178
Muses 16, 19
Mysteries 56, 63, 65, 74, 87, 90, 93, 103, 112, 135, 140, 147, 148, 149, 153, 156, 157, 176, 177, 178, 196
Mysticism 61, 94, 98, 119
Mythos 51, 55, 56, 64, 65, 102, 139, 140, 145, 147, 152, 155

N

Namaah 77
Neith 74, 91
New Dimensions 52
New Moon 114
Noel, Gerard 52

O

Old Covenant 66, 80, 85
Old Hob 32
Old Horn God 135
Old Horn King 66, 71, 83
Omphalos 70, 77, 81, 92, 101, 170
Oscalum infame 38
Osiris 70, 82, 130, 177, 181
Otz Chim 84, 85, 87, 95, 100, 159, 162

P

Pagan Dawn 52
Palaeolithic 83
Pale-Faced Goddess 59
Pan 114, 115, 116, 117, 118, 119, 120
Paracelsus 27, 181
Pellar 55
Pentagram 100, 134
Phanes 114, 115, 116, 117, 170
Phoenicians 82
Phyllomancy 74
Pickinghill 40, 190
Pistis Sophia 89, 152
Pleiades 16, 17
Plough 16, 19
Poison 57, 69, 175, 180
Poisoned Chalice 7, 50, 182
Priapus 117
Prometheus 98, 115, 177
Providence 23, 37, 42, 100, 120
Psychic News 51
Puck 29, 43

Q

Qutub, 94

R

Ragnarok 144
Reformation 24, 34
Regency 50
Riddles 61
Robin Hood 40
Roebuck in the Thicket 189, 192
Romany 30, 39
Ruach 101

S

Saxon 44, 85
Seth 77, 138, 139, 165
Shakespeare 29, 187, 188
Shekinah 75, 86, 93, 95, 100, 103, 104, 146, 164, 180, 194
Shin 64, 95, 102, 158
Sidhe 43
Simulacra 67, 97
Smith 41, 42, 50, 78, 134
Song of Amergin 103
Sophia Prounicos 77
St Dunstan 44, 45
St. Michael 38
Stang 7, 66, 70, 71, 72, 73, 78, 83, 85, 86, 89, 90, 91, 92, 93, 94, 97, 99, 100, 102, 103, 104, 111, 138, 195
Stella Maris 71, 100
Sufi 95, 175
Summoner 44
Supernal Triangle 94
Superstition 31, 35, 61, 128
Suzerainty 30, 35, 39, 145, 148, 149, 150, 189

T

Tam Lin 34
Tanist 15, 94, 102, 136, 137, 139, 196
Thyrsus 102, 119
Tiamat 167
Time 2, 66, 83, 84, 106, 107, 108, 109, 110, 111, 112, 132, 164, 165, 180
Toad bone 28, 42
Toadmen 28
Tree of Life 66, 67, 73, 75, 79, 82, 84, 91, 94, 96, 99, 101, 130, 155, 162, 181
Triangle
  Astral 94
Trimurti 135
Truth 54, 58, 59, 60, 63, 65, 77, 83, 86, 87, 89, 90, 92, 94, 100, 101, 106, 111, 112, 113, 119, 123, 124, 130, 146, 151, 152, 153, 156, 157, 175, 178, 180, 183, 185
Tubal Cain 24, 39, 50, 73, 104, 111, 135, 185
Tubalo 39

U

Underworld 2, 16, 75, 79, 84, 144
Unio Mystica 163
Upanishads 89

V

Virtue 16, 39, 46, 66, 67, 71, 73, 78, 80, 81, 83, 86, 91, 99, 103, 104, 111, 139, 146, 147, 148, 150, 152, 155, 159, 168

W

Wanderer 119
White Goddess 54
Wild Hunt 111
Wilson, Joe 16, 17, 50, 52, 56, 57
Winds 16, 17, 77, 86, 111, 115
Witch 58, 193
Witchcraft Research Association 52
Woden 42
Wyrd 91, 186

Y

Yahweh 139
Yaldaboath 138
Yggdrasil 69, 85, 90, 94, 98, 99, 143, 193
Young Horn King 71, 90, 92

The Star-Crossed Serpent Vol I

Dual-authorship of the Clan of Tubal Cain's Legacy defining 50 years of its organic evolution. Originating from within an unpublished ms written by Evan John Jones, the former Magister of the Clan since Robert Cochrane's death in 1966, it serves Testament to the Will of Fate and Tenacity of Spirit here expressed, from its inception under Robert Cochrane through Evan John Jones' own record of the Clans beliefs and practises to those of the Current bearers of this mantle, depicting the interweaving of Wyrd in the vital process of its existence and continuity in Troth to its Tutelary Spirit: The Star-Crossed Serpent

Order direct from
Mandrake of Oxford, PO Box 250, Oxford, OX1 1AP (UK)
Phone: 01865 243671 (for credit card sales)
Prices include economy postage
online at - www.mandrake.uk.net, Email: mandrake@mandrake.uk.net

www.ingramcontent.com/pod-product-compliance
Ingram Content Group UK Ltd.
Pitfield, Milton Keynes, MK11 3LW, UK
UKHW021706060326
468710UK00013B/202/J